Efficiency Criteria
for Nationalised Industries

Efficiency Criteria
for
Nationalised Industries

A STUDY OF THE MISAPPLICATION OF
MICRO-ECONOMIC THEORY

by

ALEC NOVE

UNIVERSITY OF TORONTO PRESS

First published 1973 in Canada and the United States by
University of Toronto Press   Toronto and Buffalo

ISBN   0–8020–2088–7

Printed in Great Britain
in 11 point Times Roman type
by Unwin Brothers Limited
Old Woking, Surrey

Preface

This little book originated with my concern with what appeared to be perverse decisions and illogical criteria in British national-ised industries. My own professional specialisation was in planned economies of the Soviet type, and I could discern certain common problems, especially when these economies began seriously to contemplate decentralisation. The first attempts to put the resultant thoughts on paper led to an article in the *Economic Journal* (Vol. LXXIX, Dec. 1969), and a more popular article in *New Society*. This led to discussions in seminars in various universities in Britain and America, and also in Prague and Moscow (where I discovered that the Russians had at that time no conception of 'external economies' and had no words in their language to express the concept). I was then compelled to read more of the relevant western literature, and this confirmed my belief that some longer and more coherent attack was needed on both theory and practice, out of which (I hope) some good might come. Theory could perhaps be amended to make its practitioners better able to give correct advice to politicians and business men.

This is partly a critique of micro-economics, through ana-lysing its application to public enterprise in Great Britain, and partly a challenge to the principles and criteria which have come to be accepted by the Labour and Conservative parties for the management of nationalised industries. The connecting link between the two objectives of the present work lies not only in the subject matter, nationalised industries, but also in the fact that the politicians' confusions on how nationalised industries should be run are a result of the advice of con-ventional micro-economists. It is the author's hope that the resultant discussions will also throw light upon dark corners of the economics of socialism, and also on problems facing reformers in Hungary, Yugoslavia and the USSR. Finally, perhaps this work will focus attention on the misleading, and often negative, effects of modern micro-economics on the minds

7

of intelligent men, and will lead to some reassessment of what this branch of economics ought to be doing.

If by any chance the book is free from gross errors of fact or of judgment, this is due to the generous help received from several colleagues at Glasgow University. In particular Diane Dawson and Tony Gillender read through an earlier draft and made a large number of valuable criticisms and suggestions; I also benefited from many discussions with Malcolm MacLennan. To them go my grateful thanks. I also learned much from critics at seminar discussions and from many of the works quoted in the pages that follow. No one but myself is responsible for the errors that remain.

Contents

Pure theorists sometimes take a suspicious attitude to 'structuralists' and 'institutionalists'. They prefer a theory so pure as to be uncontaminated with any material content.

JOAN ROBINSON

Grau, teurer Freund, ist jede Theorie,
Und grün des Lebens goldner Baum.

GOETHE

Chapter 1

Diagnosis

Why should anything be nationalised?
There could be two types of answer: one concerns ideology and the class war, and the other economic and/or social efficiency. In this work I shall concentrate on efficiency, i.e. on the proposition that things which are nationalised are so because in some way they can be better run than by private enterprise. This is not to dispute the validity or otherwise of the value judgment that capitalists or landlords ought to be expropriated, or that the given distribution of income or of property is wrong. Those who hold such views are entitled to hold them. (These same people may also argue that, in certain cases, private ownership of property stands in the way of efficiency.) Be all this as it may, I am assuming that the main, or a main, reason for nationalisation is the conviction that the post, transport, mines, electricity, television and gas industries are operated more efficiently, in something which could be called the public interest, under nationalisation.[1] Indeed, it is obviously in the public interest that they be operated efficiently, for otherwise the resultant waste of resources deprives the community of additional goods or services, or leisure, which it otherwise would enjoy. The problem, as we shall see, is how to identify just what efficient operation is and what criteria are applicable. However, we must forget naive 'pseudo-socialist' notions that accounting and economic operation are somehow unimportant. Nonetheless, the words 'in the public interest' were not used idly earlier in this paragraph. Unless they do have some meaning, there really is little point in public ownership of anything, and the meaning, if any, surely relates to possible conflict between private profitability and some apparently desirable act or omission. For if the question were purely one of

11

private profitability, any individual or firm, Joe Bloggs or Bloggs Ltd, could produce the goods or perform the service, and there would be no problem and no economic case for public ownership.

In the formal world of micro-economics there is some recognition of this. Public ownership, or public regulation of private business, even quite orthodox textbooks will tell you, can be justified where there is a natural monopoly, or where the existence of economic or social external effects is sufficiently important to make micro-profitability a misleading criterion. A familiar example, which appeared in textbooks already fifty years ago, is the smoking factory chimney. To abate the nuisance may reduce profits, but the smoke imposes costs on individuals who are not engaged in economic transactions with the firm which owns the factory, but who are entitled to protection. Or society as a whole gains, economically and socially, from the delivery of correspondence to all the inhabitants of the given country; members of society wish to be able to write to anyone, and have these letters delivered; but delivery of letters to remote destinations would not 'pay', save at prohibitive rates, and so in all countries the postal service has been run by the state.

Economists will generally admit that there are many instances of external economies and diseconomies, and historians will certainly recall that the economic effects of the Union Pacific Railroad, or of the railway which linked the Ukrainian wheat-fields with Odessa, were by no means limited to the profit and loss account of the respective railways and of their immediate customers.

However, some economists have the regrettable habit of forgetting the assumptions upon which their own generalisations rest. A recent example in another connection is E. J. Mishan. An original and challenging thinker, he very properly reminds us of the external diseconomies of growth, such as congestion and pollution. Yet he proves that he can wear blinkers as well as anyone. Thus in his *Twenty-one popular economic fallacies*[2] Mishan tells us that immigration cannot help our economy, nor the brain drain harm it, because men are paid the value of their contribution to the economy! If this were indeed so, an immigrant would be paid what he produces, and then, assuming he remits some of his earnings abroad and has above-average calls on social services, his net contribution is a minus. A skilled engineer who leaves Britain for Australia was paid what *he* produced, and so no net loss follows from his departure. QED.

Now this is, or can be, nonsense. One reason is that formal theory only asserts that the *marginal* labourer or engineer is paid the value of his product, or gets 'the rate for the job', and there is no particular reason to assume, in real-world conditions, that the individual who arrives or departs *is* the marginal labourer in this sense. (Not everyone who gets 'the rate for the job' is of equal skill.) However this would hold true only in equilibrium, a condition without bottlenecks of labour or of anything else, in which supply and demand for all things are equal, and where there is perfect mobility and substitutability of all factors. Furthermore, even in pure theory no one would employ the marginal labourer or engineer unless, by so doing, he obtained an income equal to the going rate of interest; otherwise it would pay him to let the money earn that interest. However, the essential point, which makes this instance of economists' blindness relevant to our theme, is that Mishan of all people forgets about external effects. By this, in the context of labour, I mean the effect of one man's work on that of others.

A simple example: a centre-half of a professional football team is paid a wage. However, apart from the contract between his club and himself, he has an effect on the performance of other players in his team. To some extent this would be reflected in his wage, but it is unlikely to be so in its entirety, because football is a team game and the separate contribution of each player cannot be readily disentangled and identified. So much so that some football teams pay the same wage to all regular first team members. It is intuitively obvious that the loss (or gain) due to the departure (or arrival) of a centre-half will not necessarily be measured by the wage of the individual in question. It will have some 'external' effects on the performance of the team.

Workers, engineers, research laboratories, are also engaged in varying degrees of teamwork. The same argument applies.

There are specificities, complementarities and the like. Trades are not interchangeable; one man's speciality affects the performance of fellow-workers. An employee performing task A requires the co-operation of someone else who can perform task B, which requires a different skill. If the man who is able to perform task B leaves, it may be difficult to replace him, and this would affect the productivity of the first employee. So clearly the departure or arrival of an employee can have effects which cannot be ignored. Therefore, *pace* Mishan, we are not wrong if we surmise that Germany has gained something from importing $2\frac{1}{2}$ million workers from abroad, something greater than their earnings, and that skilled engineers who leave Britain for Australia could represent a net loss for the one, a net gain for the other.[3]

Mishan's error is an interesting one, because it is logically on a par with the kind of error we will again and again be encountering. Because micro-economic theory is usually presented so that external effects, complementarities, indivisibilities and the like, are inconvenient (they mar the beauty of the theory), they are relegated to footnotes and all too often forgotten. The theory, and the concept of optimum with which it is associated, operates elegantly and rigorously when there is infinite divisibility, and when each transaction is, so to speak, sufficient unto itself and affects no other individual, or firm, or transaction. Then what 'pays' is, almost by definition, the right and efficient thing to do. We shall be examining the theory and its assumptions in detail in due course. It is enough to stress at this stage that this theory *fragments*. It neglects systems of inter-relationships. We have seen how Mishan misapplied micro-theory to labour. His colleagues all too readily misapply it to nationalised industries, and the cause of the error is the same: the almost instinctive search for unrelated *marginal fragments* out of which they build a concept of efficiency and rationality. (Strictly speaking, these are not unrelated; they are related *only* through market and price.) To say this is not to attack the marginal principle as such, for decisions do in fact very often concern increments of an output or a process, and thus are marginal. 'Marginal' need not imply 'fragmented'.

However, as we shall be arguing later, there are logical and indeed mathematical reasons why it in fact often does so.

Where do nationalised industries come in? How can the Mishan error analysed above apply to them? It can do so all too easily. Just as the relationship between the productivity and pay of the marginal labourer can be seen through blinkers, which do not permit even the intelligent observer to consider the effect of one labourer's work upon that of others, so a nationalised ship or bus can be deemed to be operating economically only if it makes a profit at least equal to some defined rate of return on the capital which it represents. Therefore, to cite but one example at this stage, the nationalised Scottish Transport Group removes cruise ships from the Firth of Clyde or buses from rural routes, without considering the effect this might have on the economics of tourism in Scotland, or indeed the costs which its decision might impose on other public authorities (for example, posts, education and the like). In ignoring such matters, the Transport Group can refer to the Transport Act of 1968, passed by a Labour government! Admittedly, as we shall see, the Act did make provision for subsidies, but it lends itself all too easily to a 'commercial' interpretation.

One is entitled to ask: if a public authority operating transport services does not take into account the economic (not to say social) effects of its actions, but confines its attention to its own profit and loss account (and fragments even there, as we shall see), what conceivable reason can there be for putting transport under public ownership? Who has ever doubted that transport, of all things, has external effects?

It is even said (and it could be true) that the profits of the bar on cruise ships are paid into a separate account, and are not allowed to 'count' in computing the profitability of a shipping service. It is supposed to make a profit on its purely shipping role, while drinks are a matter for the catering department. This could be so, because it is entirely consistent with the advice the 'marginal-fragmentation' economists would give. Transport is transport and drinks are drinks. The latter could be 'hived off' to private enterprise, were it not for the bar's physical

15

location in a nationalised ship, but analytically the bar *is* 'hived off'. To use its profits to offset operational losses is 'cross-subsidisation', i.e. unsound economically. Now a bar on a ship (or in a cabaret, for that matter) is not really an externality, since it is part of the same undertaking as well as being physically located there. So this is an example not of external effects but of *internal* effects.

Economic theory is, of course, aware of the existence of external effects. External economies confer benefits on persons or firms who are not the subject of the given decision, or parties to the given transaction. External diseconomies harm such individuals or firms. We will have many occasions to quote examples in the pages that follow. Actions by some individuals (or groups) can affect the productive potential or welfare of other individuals (or groups). Sometimes it is possible to reconcile these 'contradictions' through the market. Thus, to take an example, if a building operation makes a loud noise, which could be abated at a cost of £x, the residents of the area could pay the construction company this sum to reduce the nuisance. Alternatively, if the residents had legal means of redress (by suing the company for the nuisance created), it might pay the company to incur this cost. Theory also knows of complementarities, both in productive processes and in consumption. Thus Lancaster[4] has pointed out that goods are bundles of characteristics which cannot always be separately priced. Yet it is still true that students can take good honours degrees, read all the best textbooks, and still neglect these aspects of economic reality, for reasons to be discussed later on.

Indeed, the term 'externality' is of its nature ambiguous. It depends on what one is considering. If two individuals make a deal, any other individual affected by it is external to that transaction. If a factory pollutes a river, that is an external diseconomy. But if the factory itself owns fishing rights in the river, it is an *internal* diseconomy, for now we are considering an economic unit which could be defined as Factory-and-fishing. We can say that such a unit 'internalises' what would otherwise be the *external* effects of industrial waste on fish. Similarly, a shipping service to a holiday island, if its operators have no

financial interest in the island's hotels, is financially indifferent
as to the effects of its services on these hotel's profits. They are
external to its operations (though of course the hotels' existence
does contribute to demand for shipping services). But it is
perfectly possible for the hotels to be owned by the shipping
concern, or for the hotels consortium to own and operate the
ship. In either event, there is a ship-and-hotel firm, and the
externality will have been internalised. This could be rational,
because of the indivisibility-interdependency: people attracted
to the hotels use the ships, and the hotels could not make
money unless the ships took the customers to the island. In this
situation, it would be hard to identify the profits attributable
solely to ships or solely to hotels. (In practice we might have a
third of the hotels' customers travelling in their own yachts, and
half of the users of the ships will not be staying at the hotels; in
real life there are usually degrees of complementarity.)

In many countries a local authority runs ships in just the
situation here described. For example, the prosperity of the
holiday island, Ile de Ré, in the Bay of Biscay justified the
maintenance of large car ferries, fully used only at peak holiday
periods and certainly not 'paying their way' *qua* car ferries. They
are operated by the Charente Maritime *département*. It is
probable that, seen as an economic unit, the island-tourism-and-
car-ferries complex pays handsomely, though the ferries'
accounts do not show it.

Why do I dwell at such length on externalities? Because one
of the principal arguments for public operation and control of
any sector of the economy is that it permits the *internalisation of
externalities*. Indeed, this is what 'taking the public interest into
account' means. Thus the Scottish Transport Group's *raison
d'être* should be that it can take these things into account,
whereas separate private bus and shipping companies cannot.
Instead we have fragmentation even of the Transport Group's
own decision-making. Not just the bar, either. I well remember
the voice on the telephone coming to me from the Glasgow
office of a transport undertaking under the Group: 'Yes, this
[shipping] service is now withdrawn. It is a pity. It messes up one
of our own most popular tours. But you see, it is the new

accountancy.' A classic example of the *externalising of internalities*, a wilful refusal to see the wood for the trees, a marginalist fragmentation of which no intelligent businessman would be guilty, committed in the name of a misunderstood economic 'rationality'.

It is important here to avoid confusing three points, all of importance in the present context but different analytically. One relates to the negative consequences of the excessively fragmented view of profitability, consequences negative from the standpoint of economic profitability. The second concerns the question of goods and services which do not pay on any economically reasonable definition of 'pay', but which should nonetheless be provided on social grounds (e.g. a boat service to the Outer Hebrides); this raises the question of subsidisation. Finally, there is the question of how far a monopoly should be compelled, as a condition for its existence, to undertake activities, which, *given its monopoly position*, would not pay. All these questions, which will be gone into at length in subsequent pages, are begged by the doctrine of 'commercial operation'.

So one part of the disease is failure to see those interrelationships and complementarities which constitute a principal justification of large-scale operation under private as well as public ownership. The other is an inability to comprehend the logic of monopoly.

Let us make an elementary observation. A public monopoly, if told to operate 'commercially', will tend to behave in exactly the same way as a private monopoly.

Indeed, it can be argued that it would be *worse*. The reason is this. A private monopoly is generally supervised by some sort of regulating body, to prevent abuse of its position. Thus in Britain we had the Railway and Canal Commission; in America, they still have the interstate Commerce Commission and similar organisations. There are imposed statutory duties in some instances. If the monopoly is based on legal enactment, it was considered normal, even at the height of *laissez-faire*, to bind it with various conditions. Thus in 1844 it was laid down that a 'Parliamentary train' should travel along every railway, calling at every station and charging no more than a penny a

18

mile third class. Private monopolies, which are not based on law or franchise, are always conscious of being monopolists on sufferance, since failure to give some minimum satisfaction to customers could lead to the invasion of their 'territory' by a competitor.

By contrast, a public 'commercial' monopoly is subjected to few constraints, at least in Great Britain. It is told to make money, and the ministry deliberately refrains from interfering with its day-to-day operations. It must therefore be expected to behave as a private unsupervised monopolist would, if in addition he was protected by law from competition.[5] Indeed, many large private corporations are concerned with public goodwill, if only because they do not want to give politicians a justification for interference. Some of them therefore are prepared to spend a lot in order to establish a public-spirited image. Nationalised industries cannot fear nationalisation, and in addition may be barred by their own rules from spending money other than for their own business needs. This is surely a deplorable distortion of any conceivable principles of nationalisation. It should be welcomed by Conservative ideologists anxious to prove the inefficiency of 'socialism', but it is more difficult to explain the adoption of such principles by the Labour party.

Perhaps the dangers are hidden from their economic advisers by the deficiencies of monopoly theory of the conventional kind. Generations of students are taught that a monopolist would try to equate marginal revenue with marginal cost, while under competition marginal revenue would tend to equal price (we shall see later how totally ambiguous these apparently simple phrases are). The monopolist's output would therefore tend to be somewhat smaller, the price somewhat higher, than would obtain under competition, the size of the difference being dependent on demand and supply elasticities.[6]

However, like so much of micro-economics, all this is one-dimensional and over-simplified. It assumes, for instance, a totally homogeneous 'product'; it ignores quality, punctuality, goodwill, service, choice. Let me illustrate. Suppose that razor blades are a public monopoly, and the operational criterion is the volume of profit, perhaps modified by some sort of output or turnover target. What possible economic interest can the nationalised razor blade firm have in making their blades sharp? Indeed, profit and turnover alike might benefit from blades which have to be thrown away after three shaves. Under competition, it pays to be sharper than the other manufacturers. Under a public monopoly, blades will not be sharp unless there is either a moral or imposed duty, because without competition the extra cost of making them sharp becomes 'avoidable'.

'Duty' or 'purpose' are words almost unknown to micro-economics. Yet we shall show that without them nationalised industries cannot sensibly operate, nor can their function be adequately defined. (In recent years, the trend has been towards reducing drastically the obligations of British nationalised transport).

Let us proceed. A bus makes more money if passengers are crowded than if there are empty seats. A shop operates more 'economically' (more turnover per employee, less cost as a percentage of turnover) if customers stand in line. Indeed a queue always pays the supplier of any goods or service, unless the customer can go elsewhere. Good service of any kind incurs a cost, and the corresponding gain is goodwill. This word is also almost unknown to micro-economic theory, though business-men know of its importance. It is unknown because it is inconsistent with marginalist fragmentation. It asserts that what is done in one transaction affects other transactions, providing a good reason for not regarding each in isolation.

Poor service can take many forms, from failure to provide goods or services when people want them to mere indifference and rudeness. Of course, to be able to provide things when needed one must carry stocks, have reserve capacity. Stocks and reserve capacity involve costs. In theory, competition compels good service (in practice too, sometimes). Nationalised monopoly is not compelled to provide this, unless either it takes pride in the efficient fulfilment of its task (moral incentive), or its operational criteria are defined to encourage the carrying out of the purpose for which the public enterprise has been brought into being.

20

Ah, the orthodox might reply, all this overlooks an important point. Nationalised undertakings are not profit maximisers. They are supposed to achieve a norm. A very high profit is bound to lead to pressure to cut prices. Advocates of marginal cost pricing would hold that in their price policy they apply the rules of competition, not of monopoly. This is true, but it makes little difference. It is no sort of incentive to efficiency. Indeed, if poor service earns the required 10 per cent why bother to achieve an improvement? In any case, a little slackness will always ensure that profits do not rise too high. In the real world, inertia is a powerful force. Even competition is not able to combat it at times.

It is not here asserted that nationalised industries are in fact very badly run. In the first place, pride in quality and in service have survived despite the emphasis on the profit and loss account as the overriding criterion. Secondly, really outrageous neglect can give rise to pressure, public inquiry and ministerial interference. Finally, some nationalised industries are operating under severe competition, sometimes from other nationalised industries as well as private enterprise: gas and electricity are obvious examples. So, whatever the deficiencies of doctrine, the spur to good performance is often there. In theory, and to some considerable extent in practice too, economic provision of what the public wants, or can be persuaded to want, follows from the existence of competition.

Only it does not follow in the way presented in the textbooks.

Before plunging into deficiencies of theory, let us look at more instances of its misapplication in the public sector, to demonstrate to the sceptic that we are dealing with a real problem.

Docks They must 'pay'. Investment in them ought to yield the appropriate rate of return. Students are told that, strictly speaking, it is better to operate with discounted cash flow (DCF) in assessing the profitability of investments, in this as in all other public-sector projects. That is to say, the expected flow of cash benefits over the next few years is discounted to present values at some given rate of interest. It must be surmised that a negative present value would show that the project under consideration is undesirable, that it would make a loss. Of course, some docks are unsuccessful, and we had the recent instance of the semi-bankrupt Mersey Docks and Harbour Board. Its financial results may indeed be an index of high-cost inefficient operation, feather-bedding, overpaid dockers, old-fashioned management; these are all undesirable phenomena. But a very important point is ignored; modern docks have profound effects on their own hinterland. They are a clear instance where very considerable external effects are to be expected. Of course it does not follow that large losses are to be tolerated. But an examination of the investment decisions leading up to the modernisation of Antwerp, Hamburg and Rotterdam will certainly show that those who took these decisions were concerned with the economic development of the Antwerp, Hamburg and Rotterdam areas, and not only with the profit and loss account of the docks themselves. If public ownership of docks is to make any sense at all, this *must* surely be so? Not, it seems, in Britain, and the problem as such is not faced by those economic theorists who advise ministers on criteria appropriate to nationalised industries. Matters were made worse when interest rates were greatly raised, and the docks were thus given financial targets which compelled a sharp rise in costs. The higher rate of return was imposed on existing assets, as well as on new investments, by the simple expedient of making the dock authorities repay past indebtedness, incurred at an interest rate of around $3\frac{1}{2}$ per cent, by new borrowing at 9 per cent. So much for 'let bygones be bygones'!, the theory that asserts that the best use of capital assets today is, or ought to be, unaffected by their initial cost. Of course, even the most orthodox analysis recognises that the docks serve the hinterland, in the same sense in which any goods or service has customers. Orthodox analysis, however, does tend to obscure the fact that the advantages of modern dock facilities may show themselves in the profit accounts of firms very far removed from the docks themselves. Certainly the plans for the rebuilding of Rotterdam and Hamburg docks facilities consciously take into account those 'spread' effects.

The post office How on earth did the Labour party come to turn it over to a 'commercial' corporation? Competition is virtually non-existent. The external effects, on people and on business, are self-evident. Why, one might ask, is the Post Office a government department in virtually every country of the world? Why was it made a government department in Britain herself at the height of *laissez-faire*? One might have thought that the answers to these questions were self-evident too; acts which benefit the net revenue of the post office frequently conflict with other important interests. Thus the rate charged for printed matter affects business and exports. Both business and politics benefit even from the circulation of a country's press abroad. The presence of French, German, American and Italian publications on Latin American book-stalls may be due to the low postal rates from these countries compared with the British rates.

It is quite possible that the extra costs imposed on business by the two-tier post introduced in 1968 exceed the extra new revenue which it yields to the post office by a wide margin. In these and other instances, it is (or used to be) the job of the ministry to weigh the gains and losses and decide accordingly. In other words, the Post Office as a government department was able to make a cost-benefit analysis, under conditions in which costs and benefits frequently fail to find reflection in the Post Office's own accounts; it also had the power to act accordingly. The whole point of cost-benefit analysis is that one tries to value those costs and benefits which do not enter into the profit-and-loss account. Were it otherwise, it would be superfluous. It is far from clear how this is to be reconciled with principles of commercial operation, as we shall see.

The creation of the autonomous corporation, with explicitly 'commercial' criteria, is an almost classic example of confused thinking. One is at a loss to discover the reasoning of a Labour government, of its advisers, in favouring this solution. The controversy affecting the Post Office, involving the dismissal of Lord Hall in 1971, is irrelevant to the main issue of economic administration, since Lord Hall, before his departure, laid great stress on 'commercial' criteria of operation.

Efficiency Criteria for Nationalised Industries

In November 1971 the post office corporation announced a plan to reduce the quantity and quality of its services, to raise its charges and to reduce its staff. Increased charges are indeed inevitable in view of the inflationary rise in costs, but it would seem to be no one's job to contrast the savings to the post office with the loss imposed on the community through a worsening of its services. The commercial rules imposed by a bemused Labour government remove such considerations from the post office's own operating rules. In this instance, under a Conservative government, a strong protest by the Post Office Users' Council was upheld by the minister, contrary to the spirit of Labour's legislation, a fact which has created a major contradiction, not foreseen in the legislation, between the financial 'commercial' obligation of the Post Office and government policy. (The same has happened in other nationalised industries as part of the government's effort to hold back inflationary price rises.) A letter to *The Times* also raised the question, whether it is rational to adopt a plan to reduce employment, as part of a reduction of the service itself, at a time of serious unemployment. A currently fashionable philosophy would regard this as quite irrelevant to efficiency. Yet is this not just one example among many of the possible inconsistency between the profit and loss account and a properly conceived economic welfare? (Nor is this the worst part of the Post Office story; see page 88.)

BOAC At the time of writing, the public argument concerns the setting up of a rival private airline. But it was years earlier that BOAC abandoned its South American services because 'they did not pay'. The following European 'flag' airlines maintained theirs; Air-France, Lufthansa, KLM, Sabena, SAS, Alitalia, Swissair. . . . Their arguments were that it pays to be a *world* airline and to be known as such, and there are clear beneficial ('external') effects for their country's business to have the 'flag' airline operating to Brazil, Argentina, Chile, countries with a great potential whose traffic and commerce are bound to expand in the future. Note that these arguments concern both internal and external economies; a (possibly temporary) loss on

24

the South American services was good for the airline's image and would benefit its own other (profitable) services, and the effects of withdrawal would have adverse effects on other businesses in their country. In the first instance BOAC paid insufficient attention to its own commercial interests by succumbing to the disease of fragmentation ('It does not pay; cut it'). In the second, it behaved in a manner inconsistent with its *raison d'être* as a national airline, and in so doing strengthened the hand of those who sought (for perhaps irrelevant ideological reasons) to break its monopoly of British inter-continental services. If it considers itself free to choose routes that pay regardless of more general economic considerations, why should it have a monopoly position? Why have a nationalised airline at all, indeed?

Of course it does not follow that routes making losses should never in any circumstances be abandoned! Only that the decision cannot logically be based only on the accounts of BOAC. How many economists have pointed this out? How many, on the contrary, have produced theories and given advice which has the effect of making the wearing of blinkers rational?

British Rail The terms of reference of its management are now exclusively commercial. There is no duty to run any service, except that the closure of passenger lines requires the consent of the minister. They are given *carte blanche* to charge whatever the market can bear. The duty of 'common carrier', the duty of non-discrimination, the practice of a standard charge according to distance for passenger traffic, all have gone, considered old-fashioned and irrelevant to efficiency. It is not for British Rail to consider the effects of its decisions on manufacturing industry, on regional policy, on tourism. While these lines are being written, British Rail is reputed to have refused to collaborate in providing rail services to the new London fruit and vegetable market; it felt no sense of obligation, no duty to collaborate with the local planning agencies, under circumstances in which a privately-owned rail undertaking may well have felt obliged to take a more positive view. Why, one may ask, have nationalised railways, if their terms of reference are so inward-looking? Thus the measure of their efficiency is dissociated from the very purpose of their existence. Or rather it is assumed that the railways' accounts will reflect the degree to which they are carrying out its purpose.[7] My colleague Mr Gillender points out that a change of philosophy is visible in the wording of railway legislation. The 1953 Act contained the words, 'It shall be the general duty of the Commission . . . to provide railway services *for* Great Britain.' The 1962 Act put it differently, speaking of a 'duty of the Railway Board in the exercise of their powers under the Act to provide railway services *in* Great Britain.' [Emphasis mine]. One little step away from the concept that public utilities are *for* the public!

Here again, as in the case of BOAC, one must distinguish between possible effects of fragmentation on the railways' own interests, and the external effects. One must distinguish, too, the related but separate point of the proper way for a 'commercial' public body to use its monopoly powers.

At the time of the Beeching report (1963), there was no doubt that railway mileage was excessive, and some pruning had to be. Some lines were little used, with trains carrying a handful of passengers. A connecting bus would have done as well, at lower costs. However, oddly enough the railway management in recent years saw no point in ensuring that any connection in fact existed. It was the Ministry which insisted on there being buses. It is as if accountants calculated that only main line traffic paid, oblivious of the fact that the ultimate destination of passengers or goods may be off the main line, and that it is of interest to the railway that they complete their journey. Indeed, one of the most difficult problems of accounting is to assign revenues to a section of a system, precisely because a system abounds in interdependencies. Systems or network analysis are concepts well known in other spheres, such as business organisation, but they have hardly been allowed to enter the rarified atmosphere of micro-economic theory. The point is that the separate profitability of a part of a system cannot be measured save in the context of the whole. A firm is, in one of its aspects, a system of activities. The manager who wants every part of his system to pay may end up with an overall deficit; just so, a Scottish building materials firm decided only to deliver when it was profitable for it to do so, and the word got around; this firm cannot be relied upon to supply materials that are needed when they are needed. Goodwill was lost. Badwill was generated. Profits disappeared.

Something like this has been achieved by British Rail with goods traffic. No longer bound by common carrier obligations, it has acquired a reputation for picking and choosing. Anxious to minimise the number of unused wagons, it has cut back spare capacity, so that urgent loads to catch ships at ports may not get there in time. The word gets round. Lorries are bought, and are then used at times when the railways would be glad to have business. Yet the management can achieve this result by strict adherence to what seem to be textbook criteria. If investment in extra wagons, used only at peak periods, does not bring in a return (or an appropriate DCF), then it would appear not to be economically sound to provide them. Long trains with full loads are economical, and it is indeed the case that small loads for small firms can be carried more economically by lorry. There must also be a limit on the stock on little-used or unused rolling-stock. It is a matter of judgment, of balancing obligations, goodwill, the fact of inevitable peaks and troughs in demand, with the additional costs incurred. A wise management does this. Analytical fragmentation of the problem hinders it in its task.

This causes loss because there are alternatives. Railways face competition. Were this otherwise, there would be no loss of custom, and the profits would still be there, the losses being borne by the customer. It is the existence of competition which, presumably, serves as a justification for abandoning 'common carrier' duties and other regulations which protected the users in days gone by.

But competition operates unevenly. Thus there are planes that fly from London to Glasgow, and a fast road from Glasgow to Edinburgh, but neither exist between (say) Leeds and Hull, or London and Plymouth. Or one cannot get to work daily from Haywards Heath to London except by train. Or lobsters require rail transport from a Scottish port to London hotels. Or, finally, there is a great rush on the part of many families to get to Devon for the August holidays. In all the instances quoted above, current doctrine is that the management ought to use their bargaining power and charge what the market will bear.

It may be that such behaviour is commercially counter-productive, and it certainly does not generate goodwill to be asked to pay a supplement for travelling to Devon at holiday times. But let us suppose that the net effect of such practices is financially positive. Are they tolerable in a nationalised industry? Suppose the old Great Western Railway Company had decided to charge its customers extra at holiday time, or to increase fares 'selectively' so that on some routes it cost 30 per cent more to travel than on others over the same distance.[8] This would have been stopped, as a typical instance of the misuse of monopoly power by a private corporation. Why is it allowable if the 'offence' is committed by a public corporation? Yet exactly this course of action is recommended by the economic advisers to the Ministry of Transport and approved by the Ministry and by the former Prices and Incomes Board. Be it noted that nothing like this happens in France or Germany, though competition from planes, private cars and lorries is present there too. Anyone can see the *barême* in the Indicateur Chaix showing the fare for 50 or 100 or 200 kilometres on the French railways, regardless of the particular route. Far from charging extra at holiday times, the SNCF offer reduced-fare tickets for *congés payés*,[9] and consider it their duty to run extra trains to transport the passengers at holiday times, whereas British Rail have made it a practice to minimise the provision of extra trains and to limit the number of tickets they issue. The fact that this adds to congestion on West-country roads is (literally) none of their business.

Wait a moment, a critic might say. It is not true that social duties play no part in the 'official' British doctrine. Is there not a provision for subsidies? Both British Rail and the various nationalised road transport undertakings, while basing their operations on 'commercial' principles, can and do run services which do not pay, provided they receive a subsidy to cover the loss, either from the central budget or from a local authority.

This seems logical, but only on the surface. Needless to say, the payment of a subsidy may prove necessary. But once again one sees the disease of fragmentation, the refusal to think of a system, but rather of bits, and an obstinate inability to consider purpose.

Let us clarify this line of thought. Suppose first of all that a municipal transport authority is considering its bus routes. What should it do? It has figures about traffic, estimates of demand, knowledge of when offices, schools, factories, start and finish operations, the location of housing estates, the likely demand of housewives who go shopping, and so on. There are problems of frequency, of late and early or perhaps night buses. In other words, it considers what sort of a bus service the town requires. In considering this question, it must analyse costs and benefits; it might say to itself that greater frequency on the No. 2 bus route would incur such-and-such extra costs, which may or may not be worth while. It must also determine the appropriate basis for charges which would pay for the system of services which it is contemplating. The charges may be flat-rate, for simplicity of collection and accounting (this is so in most cities of the world, outside Britain), or they may vary by distance and perhaps by time of day ('off-peak' returns, etc). But the one thing which would surely be ridiculous is for the authority to inform the municipality that No. 2 route does not pay and that they propose to withdraw it unless subsidised 'on social grounds'. What social grounds? Subsidised by whom, exactly? What does the municipal transport department exist for? Of course, it may be decided to charge fares which do not cover cost and to subsidise the system as a whole, which happens in Paris, New York and elsewhere. But that a *part* of a transport *system* be separately subsidised by those on whose behalf the system is run? Really?

It may be thought that no one would advise such a procedure. Alas, some do. Here is Mr. Munby of Nuffield College, Oxford, giving evidence to the Select Committee: 'The first thing one would expect London Transport to do . . . would be to say which are the services which pay for themselves, which are the services which do not pay for themselves, where are the losses, and what would be a rational pricing policy with regard to costs.' If then the Greater London Council 'do not like the consequences . . . , then the question comes: how do you subsidise this particular thing?' In this way, argues Munby, you eliminate what he calls the 'grey area' in which commercial principles and social obligations uneasily coexist. He seems to desire to remove the latter from operational criteria of management. Indeed he *blames* them for 'following a policy which is explicitly stated in their Annual Reports of what they call a "social contract" in London, *which I think makes no economic or social sense at all'.*[10]

In practice in Great Britain considerable powers still reside, outside London, in the Traffic Commissioners, left over from past legislation (they were set up as long ago as 1931). They can refuse permission to abandon bus routes. Presumably Mr. Munby and those who think like him would regard this as an anachronism.

Let us pursue this further. First, a point of pure practice. If one appoints a traffic manager, surely he ought to be analysing when and where passengers wish to go, and this, subject to financial constraints, should be his primary task; (who else will have sufficient information to draw up schedules of vehicle movements, time-tables, etc?).

Secondly, if one has (say) twenty bus routes in a town, and passengers change from one bus to the other, the identification of revenues applicable to one route alone presents insuperable difficulties. In fact one tends to have system revenue rather than identifiable route revenue. The same is true of urban underground or rapid-transit networks the world over.

Thirdly, there are problems of complementarity and indivisibilities, not only of vehicles but also of passengers' journeys. Thus some of the passengers who travel outwards at 'profitable' times may wish to return to their homes late (or may be uncertain as to whether they might have to do so), and would use a car or a bicycle unless there were means of getting home at what might appear to be an 'unprofitable' time.

Fourthly, what is the point of having a municipal (or any other) bus monopoly other than for the provision of a system of transport? The logic of the dominant 'school' (say Alan Day, or Denis Munby) is to disassemble the system, to operate only the profitable parts, and to suspend any route or service unless specifically subsidised.

What, then, is left of the system? Why not make every bus a separate limited company, run for its own profit? The point is that the organisation providing the transport for an area must do its job, or else resign the task to someone else, or free it for all comers. This is no case for confining the task to a public monopoly, banishing others from competing, and then asking it to operate on so-called commercial criteria. That makes the worst of all possible worlds.

Among the few economists who take a reasonable view of all this is William A. Shepherd, who is sceptical of the virtue of what he calls 'direct subsidies for certain "social" activities of the public corporations'; he sees that 'serious problems would arise in specifying which activities are "social" and which are "commercial", and he would favour 'properly designed lump-sum payments', which is my 'subsidy to the system as a whole', with cross-subsidisation within the system as its logical corollary.[11]

In his evidence to the Select Committee, Professor Wiseman did visualise 'pirate' buses, i.e. competition. One cannot assert that the competitive solution is impossible, but it would have sizeable social costs, such as the withdrawal of services from many suburban areas, compelling the residents to use cars and to add to congestion. Presumably a public transport undertaking ought to be concerned about congestion.

Of course, the municipal or urban arguments used above apply in some measure to all forms of transport. Only occasionally, as for instance in the case of an isolated line such as Inverness-Wick, is the 'network' or 'system' problem of minor significance. No doubt the Deutsche Bundesbahn or the SNCF can and should reduce the mileage of a network inherited from the pre-car era, but they would probably be wise enough not to put on blinkers when engaged in the necessary task of pruning. A simple illustration of interdependency will suffice. Imagine for a moment a network of 10,000 miles of railway lines (or bus lines, or air lines; the logic is the same). Imagine further that they charge a standard sum per mile, and that the system as a whole just breaks even. Then, by any conceivable system of accounting, half of the lines of which the system is composed would make a profit, half a loss. How could every mile of track give the same financial result, save by the most unlikely coincidence? If one closed the half that makes a loss ('unless subsidised on social grounds'), and the remaining half broke even, then half of *this* would make a loss, and so on *ad infinitum* until the system is wrecked totally.

No doubt this is why the implementation of the Beeching plan had such disappointing financial consequences. In the years from 1963 to 1968 the route mileage fell by over 25 per cent, passenger traffic by a similar percentage, and the deficit actually rose. That is to say, one is in danger of 'wasting subsidies on an unconnected or disjointed network', yielding smaller total benefits per million pounds of subsidy in the course of an effort to cut losses by eliminating loss-making segments of the system (the figures and the cited phrase are taken from an unpublished paper by Dr D. Wiggins, of Bedford College, London). It has also been calculated that, per million of subsidy, the French transport far more people and goods than British Rail do. Given the respective philosophies, this would be scarcely surprising.

The clue to this puzzle, if it is a puzzle, is of course that the profitability of the 'profitable' lines is in some degree dependent on the traffic generated on the 'unprofitable' lines (and it follows that the use of inverted commas is mandatory, since 'profitable' is ambiguous, made so by the interdependency). Yet we have economists who insist that unprofitable lines should not be 'cross-subsidised' by the profitable ones, without showing the slightest awareness of the problem. The recommendation that each line should levy such charges as cover its cost is equally misconceived, because this would only be logical and rational on the assumption that the interdependency referred to above did not exist.

Let me illustrate this with the simplest possible example. Imagine a line with stations at A, B, C, D, E, F, and G, running from the centre (A) to the outer suburb G. As one goes further from A, less people use the line, and the train carries relatively few people between stations F and G. Yet the common overheads and joint inescapable costs being what they are, the cost of providing a service from A to B (when it is packed) is practically the same as from F to G. Consequently costs per passenger mile are much lower from A to B, let us say three times lower. Should the fare then be three times lower, to keep in step with costs? Surely not, if only because many of those who start their journey at G will travel from B to A.

The matter could be tackled in a different way also. Instead of analysing the costs in terms of pence per passenger-mile, one could take the existence of line A—G as given, and concentrate one's attention only upon the marginal costs of operating from F to G. Since most of the costs are fixed, the additional cost attributable only to running trains for one extra station are fairly small. This is the sort of approach which is similar to Vickrey's analysis of marginal cost pricing. However, an analysis of this type could apply to any pair of stations on the line, in which case revenues would not cover the very large fixed costs at all. Consequently it would surely be necessary to allocate these costs in some way. It is doubtless true that consideration of the segment of the line from F to G could only be adequately undertaken in terms of its contributions to the whole line or the whole system. This would be consistent with theory properly understood. However, how then is one to find a comprehensible basis for separate charging related specifically to the costs of operating between F and G?

Let us complicate matters a little and assume that there is a river which the line must cross, and that a bridge had to be built. Clearly costs per mile in the sector which includes the bridge must have been higher than on the rest of the line. Should one therefore charge a larger sum for those passengers who travel between that particular pair of stations? If no rail system in the world does this, could it be that they are all mistaken? Yet it has been seriously proposed that South London commuters whose journeys take them via a bottle-neck at Lewisham ought to be charged more, presumably because the cost of eliminating the bottle-neck would be considerable (even though in fact the bottle-neck is not being eliminated!), or perhaps simply by crude 'what the market will bear' logic, since there is no room on the trains. Amid all these complications, theories which attempt to fragment the pricing process land one in the gravest local difficulties.

We will be showing that these considerations, though particularly significant in transport, are of importance throughout the economy, indeed wherever one has systems of activities, interlinked processes, decision-making, all affecting parts of the whole.

The orthodox micro-economist will again demur. He will not recognise himself. Of course, he will say, when we speak of marginal revenue or marginal costs, we mean those pertaining to the whole, e.g. the net contribution of a particular line, bus, flight or whatever, to the system. Of course they, and the management, have heard of feeder services. They have heard, too, of cost-benefit analysis. There are some familiar built-in constraints: thus the post office must deliver letters also to the Outer Hebrides. Has all the foregoing then been an all-out assault on an open door? I do not think so. Mistakes of the kind analysed in the preceding pages, though not always the precise instances described, have occurred. Function, purpose and duty have been almost consigned to oblivion, and certainly appear nowhere in the investment criteria recommended for use in the public sector. Some of the errors, if made, may well represent a misapplication of orthodox theory. But in the next pages I will try to demonstrate that the theory is misleading, partly because it incorrectly describes business behaviour, partly because its practitioners tend to overlook the logic of their own (analytically legitimate) simplifications and abstractions and see real problems through a kind of distorting mirror.

If any reader doubts this, let him read through any popular textbook of economics and try to find any serious analysis of the kind of problems raised in the preceding pages. He will have to look a long time.

Chapter 2

Micro-economics and the Real World

All generalisations simplify reality. All theories are based in some degree on *ceteris paribus* assumptions, or abstract from something. Economic theories are not directly applicable to actual situations 'on the ground'. There is no reason why they should be.

So 'modern' micro-economics is not to be faulted merely by reference to the complexities of life. Marxist theory too is abstract in this sense. For example the Marxian 'law of value' assumes the constancy of many relationships which, in a dynamic reality, are not in fact constant. Thus it is assumed that profits (return on capital) are equal in all sections of the economy. The same assumption operates under equilibrium conditions in neo-classical economics. Indeed this tendency can be shown to exist. It can also be shown that profits are often unequal for a variety of reasons; risk, uncertainty, changes in demand and supply conditions. It is clear that in a dynamic world profits ought to be unequal. Capital flows into expanding industries, and supports innovation, because its owners expect above-average profits in these sectors, and capital flows out of obsolete industries, or those affected by falling demand, because profits fall or become negative. Inefficiency is likewise punished by losses; above average efficiency earns above-average profits. All of which in no way 'disproves' the proposition that profits tend to equalise themselves, *ceteris paribus*. No more does the existence of excess stocks, or of temporary non-availability of a given product, disprove the economic principle that supply tends to equal demand, unless artificially prevented from so doing.

Similarly, it is perfectly legitimate, in a theory of the firm, to abstract from the organisation of trade unions and from tariff policies. Naturally, the behaviour of any particular firm may be affected by unions and by tariffs, and indeed by the weather, fire risk, a heart attack suffered by its managing director, a bad harvest in the country supplying its raw materials, and other factors too numerous to mention. No one in his right mind would advise an actual firm what to do unless he studied the special circumstances of that firm, and these could include trouble with trade unions, foreign tariffs, etc. But the theorists are right to leave these aside while generalising about the firm as such, and they can get useful insights from doing so.

Consequently one's criticism of conventional micro-economics is not, and cannot be, based on the inevitable fact that it does not encompass all the infinite variety of life. So long, that is, as the theorist does not omit or assume away some of the key elements of the subject-matter to which he chooses to give attention, and so long as he never forgets what simplifying assumptions he has made.

'It is easy enough to make models on stated assumptions. The difficulty is to find assumptions which are relevant to reality. The art is to set up a scheme that simplifies the problem so as to make it manageable, without eliminating the essential character of the actual situation on which it is intended to throw light.'[12]

Theory can mislead, and one example was the belief in wage reduction and budget expenditure cuts as the way to combat depression. The fact that one entrepreneur's profit would certainly benefit from the reduction of his wage costs was generalised, and it just was not seen that the decrease in aggregate purchasing power resulting from a general cut in wages would have an adverse effect on business activity. It needed a Keynes to point out 'what should be obvious', but, in Keynes's own words, 'the difficulty lies not in the new ideas, but in escaping from the old ones, which ramify, for those brought up as most of us have been, into every corner of our minds'.

Micro-economics customarily rests on a series of assumptions which its practitioners only occasionally examine. It is marginal (incremental) in its approach. It is resolutely non-institutional. Firms exist, but the theory takes little interest in them; their organisation, the way in which they decide, is largely ignored. They are supposed to be profit-maximisers, though recently this is being questioned, as we shall see. It is usually silently assumed that each firm provides one good or service, and that there is no problem raised in defining this. Much of the theory is static, either ignoring time altogether, discussing a stationary equilibrium, or sometimes comparing two different equilibrium situations (comparative statics).

Suppose, then, that there is perfect competition, in the sense that every product is made by a large number of firms operating in a perfect market, in which all needed information is available. Suppose further that factors of production are mobile and substitutable. Then every profit-maximising entrepreneur would 'combine factors by setting marginal everything equal to marginal everything else',[13] to cite a refreshingly vigorous critic. Labour's wages would tend to equal its marginal product, interest would equal marginal productivity of capital, prices would equal marginal costs. The consumer would so distribute his income between alternative uses as to maximise his satisfaction, and goods and services would be provided in response to consumer demand through the market. The market for goods and for factors, and the price mechanism, would then ensure that efficiency was maximised, that an optimum was reached. This would, by definition, be a situation in which any incremental change would be for the worse. Conversely, any situation is sub-optimal in which someone can so reallocate resources as to increase net output or human satisfaction.

Micro-economics as usually taught is closely related to the concept of general equilibrium, formalised by Walras, and to the concept of 'Pareto optimality'. Welfare economics, of which all this is part, has been criticised and debated, but the basic philosophy survives only slightly dented. The reason for the attractiveness of these doctrines is their consistency and logic, and the mathematical structures which can be erected upon them. Furthermore Pareto-optimality is so defined as to escape the awkward problem of interpersonal comparisons; it is a situation in which no one can be made better off without making someone else worse off.

These doctrines are part of the basic training of thousands of economists. Sure enough, on the Pareto-Walras basis, assuming that we live in their kind of world, it is perfectly true that everything has an alternative use, and that the one which yields a higher profit is by definition the one which brings one closer to optimal efficiency. Conversely, the use of resources which yields a lower rate of return is a misuse of resources; if a higher rate is thereby foregone, an opportunity has been foregone to increase welfare. This, as we shall see, affects advice given on nationalised industries today.

All economists are aware that the real world is not a Pareto world. Competition is imperfect, there is uncertainty, factors are not all mobile or substitutable, there are indivisibilities. It is recognised, too, that the welfare of society is not solely a matter of individual consumer preference, that the pursuit of profitability can be complicated by external economies and diseconomies. The point is also made that, if some of the preconditions of optimality are absent, the application of Pareto-type rules may land one away even from second-best solutions. There is a sizeable critical literature on all this. Yet the underlying ideas continue to live, and one repeatedly encounters Pareto-optimality introduced as a species of operational criterion.

It is seldom recalled that 'Pareto' and competition are mutually inconsistent categories. A Pareto optimum is one in which all resources are fully employed, in which all firms are equally (optimally) efficient. Everyone can then go on doing the same thing for ever, or until changes occur in demand or in techniques. Competition requires spare capacity, for how else can one compete successfully? There is no spare capacity in the Pareto-Walras model. Competition also requires one to damage the interests of one's competitors, yet the very definition of Pareto optimality precludes making anyone (including one's competitors) worse off. This conception is also inconsistent with technical progress, because this almost always damages someone who has invested in a now-obsolete process.

This view of optimality is hardly reconcilable with growth or with investment. G. B. Richardson has pointed out that either imperfect information or collusion are preconditions for investment, for otherwise any entrepreneur would know that all his competitors see the same profitable opportunity that he can, and by their actions they would make it unprofitable.[14] Indeed, equilibrium and investment are barely compatible concepts. Most investments are due to imbalances, shortages which give rise to above-average profit expectations, or to the presence of some other dynamic, and hence disequilibrating, factors.

These pages were already typed when I was able to obtain Janos Kornai's remarkable book, *Anti-equilibrium*. As its title makes abundantly clear, it represents an attack on Walrasian general equilibrium models, making the same point about the incompatibility of real competition and general equilibrium that was made above. The theories which he criticises fail, in his view (and mine) to meet the criteria appropriate to a science purporting to deal with the world of facts. 'In real sciences, a theory is a systematic description of essential interrelations between the variables of reality. That is, only those theorems and propositions (deduced from assumptions not in conflict with reality) which describe the real world more or less accurately may be considered acceptable.'[15] Formal general-equilibrium orthodoxy is least able to cope with dynamic factors, above all with growth or (as we shall show at some length) with investment decisions.

Nonetheless, theorists imbued with Pareto-type concepts do discuss investment. It is assumed that its total level will reflect the 'time-preference of the community' (seen still as the sum of individuals and firms of which it is composed), this being equal to the rate of interest, which in turn is held to equal the marginal productivity of capital. Savings to the value of a given sum are forthcoming at this rate of interest, and capital will be borrowed at this rate so long as the increment which it will yield over and above consumption in the present, in the form of an additional flow of (future) goods and services, will at least equal this rate of interest. It follows that any investment which fails to yield this rate of return (or discounted cash flow) is sub-optimal, since an opportunity must presumably exist to achieve a higher yield, which would make society better off without (the theory insists) making anyone worse off. This analysis is applied also to investment projects in nationalised industries. Does a project satisfy the criterion of yielding a future return equal to what (in these inflation-prone days) is still called *the* rate of interest? Then it is worth while. Much ink has been devoted to comparing different ways of computing the future flow of benefits, and students answer examination questions and prove that Discounted Cash Flow (DCF) is a superior measure to the rate of return. Investment projects, like all else in this theory, are assumed (silently) to be divisible and adjustable to bring marginal productivity and rates of return (or DCF) to the appropriate level. (Much more on investment criteria later on).

A key element in micro-economics is the marginal principle. Since this is at the root of so much misunderstanding, it is worth dwelling on this.

In equilibrium, wages will tend to equal the productivity of the marginal labourer. Were it otherwise, it would pay the firms either to hire more labour and thereby increase profits, or to reduce their labour force with the same result. (Pareto addicts would presumably argue that dismissal is an act which does not damage the interests of the man dismissed, because in the ideal world he would be instantly re-employed.) Price under competition will tend to equal the marginal product. Suppose a factory is producing shoes, and it finds that it makes profits above zero ('zero', that is, over and above the going rate of interest). It would then pay it to increase output until marginal costs increase to equal marginal revenue. This theory has trouble with increasing returns (i.e. costs falling instead of rising when output increases), but usually evades the problem by assuming that decreasing returns are the rule. Theory does sometimes seek to cope with such exceptions, and some of its practitioners argue in favour of subsidies in such cases, because of the welfare gain which accrues if one slides further along an increasing returns curve.

Marginal productivity, marginal cost, marginal rates of substitution; the word 'marginal' recurs rather often in conventional theory. It must therefore be supposed that those who use it know what it means. Alas, this is by no means always so.

Nationalised industries, then, like efficient firms in micro-economic analysis, should seek to equate marginal revenue and marginal cost.[16] Their investment decisions should be those which presumably, assuming marginal cost pricing, would bring them an appropriate DCF at the going rate of interest. Time must come into the picture, since we speak of flows, so we are asked to accept the concept 'long-run marginal cost', which differs from current cost by having to take investment outlays into account. Though the books seldom say so, there is also a special sense in which revenues must also be seen in a kind of time-dimension. Were it otherwise, an advertised flight with insufficient passengers would simply be cancelled, thereby giving the firm an immediate benefit, but obviously such an airline would find its revenue adversely affected by such behaviour within a quite short timespan. (In seminars, I have quoted an instance of an East European bus undertaking which ordered its staff to throw off passengers and turn the bus around if, on its journey to the suburbs, the number of passengers fell below 7. I have asked, 'In what respects would such behaviour be inconsistent with our own theories?' I have seldom received a reply.)

Let us look closely at what is meant by 'margin'. In the simple 'purely-competitive' world of homogeneous products made by a large number of small firms, this may seem not to matter. Mathematically, too, it is all quite unambiguous and exceedingly convenient, hence the tenacity with which the over-simplified concept is held. The assumption of infinite divisibility, necessary to ensure the equality of marginal productivities throughout the economy, makes one suppose that marginal quantities are very small; one pair of shoes, one labourer, one machine, perhaps one span of a bridge. Pressed, the conventional theorists are apt to reply, 'Of course we do not think literally of infinite divisibility. We consider only those units which are the subject of a separate decision.' Agreed. We will not argue about the marginal passenger on a train carrying 500 people, or one spoke in the wheel of a bicycle. Let us accept that the infiniteness of divisibility is theoretical perfectionism, and deal with such units as are the subject of decision-making. This, we all agree, means that one will come up with imperfections at the edges arising from indivisibility, so that some smooth curves turn out to be staircases. But the principle survives. *As far as possible*, the marginal rule should be observed. As far as practicable, the Pareto principles should be applied, in the interests of efficiency. So the conventional theory asserts, or implies.

I do not want to suggest that 'conventional' theorists are unaware of problems raised by such theories as these. There is a sizeable literature on monopoly, monopsony, 'second best' and its implications, as well as detailed and valuable studies of problems of particular industries and firms. However, much of the 'mainstream' micro-economic theory has gone in the direction of sophisticated mathematical restatement of propositions based upon simple assumptions, and the welfare-marginalist basis survives barely touched, or is even reinforced by the methodology. Indeed, the more 'advanced' the theory, the less it seems to bear on reality. To quote a vigorous critic again, 'The more elementary the textbook is, the more likely there will be information on different organisational forms. However, as soon as our study becomes 'advanced', we do not bother to differentiate between General Motors and the local candy store'.[17]

I believe that Pareto-type concepts relate primarily to, and indeed originated in, the world of allocation, not of production. If goods already exist, then one can discuss their valuation and optimal allocation between uses without running into too many problems, except perhaps those concerned with interpersonal comparisons of utility and the effect of one man's demand schedule on another's, and other such matters which do not concern us here. Then no issues arise over decision-making in production and investment.

When production processes and investment decisions are

considered, one runs into the simple question, What is a *marginal product*? Indeed, what is a product? There is a literature on product differentiation, from which one learns that there are very large numbers of products which are, or seem to be, different, and it is appreciated that this affects the competitive model. However, it is not the existence of several nationally advertised brands of detergent or toothpaste, or car models, which should worry us, for this is still on a one-dimensional level.

Even if one were to take an unambiguous definition of a 'product', the definition of 'marginal' runs into difficulties. As Joan Robinson has remarked, 'To find the marginal product of a specific factor, say a certain type of machine, we have to consider what output would be lost if a unit of this factor were withdrawn. This loss is the reduction in output of the commodity that this machine was used to make minus the increase in output of other things due to deploying the labour and other factors cooperating with the machine in other uses. The physical marginal product is thus a very complex entity, while the value of the marginal product has no unambiguous meaning, since the pattern of prices, of factors and commodities, is altered by the change in productivity capacity.[18] But sometimes it is not at all clear what the product is, or a process of production can be divided between different firms, or different units which might be within the same corporation.

Take cars, for instance. Their manufacture requires the assembly of parts, some of which can be used in the making of other products (e.g. tractors), and could be manufactured in an integrated plant or bought in from outside sub-contractors. Spare parts are also made, and after-sales service is needed. What do we mean when we say the product 'car'?

The oil industry explores, drills, extracts, refines, transports. It is a system of interrelationships, requiring an administrative apparatus which controls a wide variety of processes, including operating tankers at sea.

At the other end of the scale, one has a service industry such as a supermarket. Does it include its own car park? Or that hotel on an island. As oil needs tankers, it needs a boat. Are we considering the hotel, or the hotel-and-boat, as the 'product' or 'service'?

Precisely because of the existence of interlinked and interdependent processes, some firms aim at vertical or horizontal integration, to internalise what would be externalities, and to increase bargaining power. Firms, then, are usually multi-product multi-process, providing a variety of goods and services in a network of interrelationships. Within the firm, these are usually of an administrative rather than a market kind? Why?

Surely because profitability of the part could be a misleading guide to efficient resource use. Looking at textbooks of microeconomics. one wonders why firms become big. Surely it cannot be 'technological economies of scale', if such firms as ICI or DuPont or Shell operate many dozens of productive units of varying size. Can they be meaningfully disaggregated, fragmented by marginal analysis designed to compute the separate profit of each of them? Sometimes they can. Some firms are able to do this, and it certainly is worth trying. However, decisions cannot be based on such computations unless one also takes into account the internal effects. The effect on the whole firm of a decision taken by a subordinate manager may be unknown to him, either because the necessary information is not available at his level (marketing and research departments are apt to be at headquarters), or because the profitability of the part can actually be in contradiction with the interests of the whole. Thus an increase in profits of tankers (or of a tanker) can have an adverse effect on refining undertaken by the same corporation. Just so the abandonment of 'unprofitable' service arrangements could damage the sale of cars, if customers learn that they cannot get the required gasket, piston-ring or piece of piping with less than two months' delay.

Which brings one to goodwill. The profit-affecting interrelationships could be part of a system of production and distribution. They could also, and frequently do also, affect technologically unrelated parts of the same firm's activities.

Thus a shop may keep lavish stocks, of footwear, food or flannels, because in its view its sort of customers expect a wide choice. 'Go to Simkins, you can get it there.' Conversely, disappointment creates badwill; 'Very poor selection; try Goldberg's.'

The effects of goodwill are sometimes surprisingly widespread, and sometimes justify considerable expense, and even industry-wide or governmental regulations. Particular planes or trains can make or mar a whole system's or even a whole country's reputation for punctuality. The Rolls-Royce affair is a striking example of the external effects of one firm's misfortunes on the standing of large segments of British industry, though they were in no sense to blame for what occurred. The quality of any Japanese car or camera reflects on the standing and saleability of Japanese cars and cameras, including those made by other firms. The French government thought it worthwhile to ban cover charges in restaurants, because they reflected adversely on tourism in France. A *fortiori*, the image projected by any set or part of a firm, can reflect positively or negatively on the profitability of the firm as a whole.

So we have both interlinked processes of production and distribution, complementarities (feeder services, a degree of joint supply or demand, etc), and the commercial impact of the activities of parts upon the whole (and of one transaction upon other transactions) through goodwill. Marginal analysis which ignores this, and treats a part in isolation, may well lead to harmful consequences in the ordinary business of business life.

I foresee two objections to all this. One would assert that orthodox theory not only recognises but insists upon the interrelationship between the parts of which the economy is composed. The other would be again to point out that marginal revenue ought indeed to be computed by reference to its impact on the whole firm.

Let us dispose of the second point by conceding it. Indeed that is what our theories ought to mean, but we very seldom convey this to students, because we present things in a one-dimensional way, with a marginal 'product' assumed to be something quite clear and unambiguous, and a marginal transaction assumed (since the contrary is not stated) to have no effect on other transactions, and to exist in a sort of isolation.

The first point is indeed important. Micro-economic theory does assert the interdependence of parts, through the market. Textbooks tell us that Walrasian general equilibrium precisely interrelates everything, being in this respect distinguished from the partial equilibrium theories of such as Alfred Marshall. Changes in demand for some goods also affect prices of other goods. Raw materials and fuels used in productive processes are also purchased through markets. Of course (the critic will say) car manufacturers need engines. And bakers need flour, and to make flour one needs wheat, in the growing of which one uses tractors, fertiliser, ploughshares and whatnot. They all affect each other. So what? Why is this a challenge to a properly understood theory? The critic could add that quite a high proportion of decisions and transactions in the real world have some external effects, but to take them fully into account would require a vast economic planning bureaucracy and be prohibitively expensive as well as inefficient.

I would reply that I accept all that. However, firms, large and small exist, and within the firms various processes are related to one another, in the main, not through the market but by administrative decision, that is by instructions, through hierarchies, and not via price-and-market type of information, or not by such information alone. When, to repeat, it pays to internalise externalities, they are (or should be) administered within a single unit. If it does not i.e. if the gains are outweighed by the costs, then of course there is no point in attempting to improve on that which is more effectively achieved through the market and the price mechanism.

But when large firms do exist and do 'internalise', then it is surely logically incorrect to unpick the package and to act as if efficiency is best achieved by simulating a situation in which the parts of which the firm is composed are themselves independent firms, and the decision which each part makes is sufficient unto itself. This is what I have called earlier the externalisation of internalities. Example: treating each bus route of an urban network as if it were a separate firm. Obviously, if the parts react upon one another, it is wrong to treat them as if they do not. Yet some insist on doing so. Mr Munby, in an article he contributed to a French journal, asserted that correct pricing in rail transport required separate computations of revenue-cost relationships in respect of every section of line, junction, station, marshalling yard. Of course this was impracticable, rough averages may have to be used, but the nearer this ideal could be approached, the better.[19] Surely this view is simply wrong.

Once again I can invoke the assistance of William G. Shepherd. He criticises the view that 'price-output decisions should be decentralised to the smallest producing units which can still realise economies of scale,' which are then 'to operate as commercial units'. His 'Munby' is, or rather are, Little and Ramanadham, but the list could be prolonged, for this is almost orthodoxy. Shepherd points to the highly artificial 'static, perfectly competitive conditions, with no private-social cost divergences', under which this approach could work out. But these 'private market rules' in fact break down in real life, and 'therefore decentralisation in a private-market model would yield an efficient allocation solution at each unit only by a very remote chance.' He also wrote, 'in fact a major gain from public ownership has been to internalise various economies external to the individual plant' (or segment of a railway network, Mr Munby!). So, 'in view of the foregoing, the vague private-market criteria and policy rules which have recently been proposed can be said essentially to comprise an empty economic box.'[20] Hear, hear! Yet still a minority voice, hardly heard.

In some cases, of course, external effects can themselves be the subject of market transactions. Thus reverting to the hotel-boat example, the boat could be separately owned, and receive a subsidy from the hotel to continue operations which it might otherwise decide to suspend. (This is the kind of rational act which, if undertaken within a single undertaking, might appear to be cross-subsidisation, a point to be taken up in a moment.)

All this introduces a considerable ambiguity into the meaning of any particular case of a margin. Let us take a 20-lecture course on economics of developing countries. Where and what is the marginal lecture? The course is a connected whole. What is the benefit conferred upon the student by lecture No. 12? The question is unanswerable because it is part of a course. Is the course then unalterable? Naturally not. It could be reduced to 15 lectures, for instance, and a good deal of the content of lecture 12 rearranged, abbreviated, omitted. But these (doubtless 'marginal') decisions only make sense in the context of the course and of the purpose the course is intended to serve.

The 20-lecture course is itself part of a larger whole, and could be omitted from the prescribed regulations. So it could be considered marginal. Its retention or omission could be discussed meaningfully only in the wider context of the degree of which it is part. Just so one tanker's journey is part of that tanker's annual schedule, and the tanker itself is one of a fleet, which is serving an oil company which is engaged in moving crude oil from the Gulf to some refinery a thousand or more miles away. Tankers are indivisible units, involving high fixed costs. What decisions can be based only on one tanker's accounts? If its best use could be so achieved, why is each tanker not a limited company of its own, thus saving on bureaucracy and administration? (In some cases, of course, tankers *are* separately owned.)

The 'pure' marginal analysis of the textbook leaves out such considerations, which apply in some degree within most firms or systems of activities. It is indeed theoretically and mathematically tidier to forget about them. But we should not forget that we have assumed them out of the way for analytical convenience, not because these are unimportant matters.

In this connection, a lot of nonsense is talked about the irrationality of cross-subsidisation. Of course, the subsidisation of loss-making by profit-making activities within the same nationalised (or private) industry *can* be irrational. But, as I pointed out at length elsewhere,[21] the terms are used very loosely indeed.

I instanced the possibly negative rate of return on assets which are used mainly as reserve capacity (e.g. spare generating plant, or reserve footballers, or aircraft standing by to ensure that all travellers wishing to fly on the shuttle from Boston to New York

can do so at a busy time). I pointed out, too, that one independent firm can subsidise another, as when one airline pays
another to help it run a feeder service from which the first
airline derives a net benefit, a payment which, if made within
the *same* airline (which could own both routes) would look like
cross-subsidisation. Marginalism can be misused, the search
for equalising rates of return in a world full of indivisibilities
and complementarities can be a nonsense.

In the case of the Boston-New York shuttle, the airline is
clearly of the opinion that the passengers' knowledge that they
can certainly board a plane on the hour pays, though it involves
them necessarily in losing money on marginal planes, these
being the ones least often used and most often kept in reserve
and for which it would be commercial nonsense to charge extra
fares. In such a case, where is the margin for purposes of
economic analysis? I am far from suggesting that this question
has no answer, only that it is not obvious and most of our
students would not know it.

Or take London Transport. Marginal cost pricing? Of what?
Of a particular bus? Of the No. 2 bus route? Of the No 2 bus
route at peak and at slack times, or after 9 pm? Of all buses
north of the river, or within 10 miles of Charing Cross, at
particular times of the day? Passengers change buses, and also
change on to railways. Revenues are interdependent. Buses are
indivisible, and are part of a system. Ignoring for a moment the
issue of duty to the public, and abstracting from the complex
problem of allocating overheads and joint costs, *what margin is
one talking about*? (Calling it 'long-term' does nothing to
simplify matters.)[22]

Confusion arises between several senses, or aspects, of
marginalism. There is, first, the stage at which a project is
being planned and alternatives are being considered. Thus a
given system (rapid-transit lines, television transmitters, gas
pipelines or whatever) could be of size x, or x + 1. The additional unit or increment would cost a certain sum to build and
operate, and would yield a revenue at some price which may be
the system price. The calculation relating to this incremental
unit may indeed be needed in order to help decide whether

x or x + 1 should be chosen. It is much harder to work x, i.e. the system, into the marginal framework, because, firstly, large systems are not incremental, and, secondly, it can land one in nonsense. Thus, to take a simple illustration, one can talk about the marginal product of a coal miner, and define this as the difference made to output by whether he is there or not. But it is not possible to talk sensibly about the marginal product of *all* miners, since, as we have seen in the coal strike, the effect of the withdrawal of their labour is so widespread as to wreck the entire economy. Thus it is hardly feasible to compare meaningfully a short-term situation with and without coal miners, or coal, and derive from this comparison any useful information about marginal productivity, incomes or price.

Once a system or firm is in operation, marginal cost will depend on the degree of utilisation of capacity. This is partly a question of uneven demand, but can be the consequence of excess capacity.

This capacity would perhaps not exist if there had been perfect foresight in the past, but it does exist. Doctrine about its optimal use is singularly muddled. On the one hand, we are told that 'bygones are bygones', the capital cost of the past is irrelevant, and pricing should relate to current operational costs and revenues. On the other, interest charges accruing as a result of past investment expenditures are usually included for purposes of deciding what prices to charge; thus, as we have seen, the docks had to pay 9 per cent and more on borrowings made in order to repay debts originally incurred (at lower interest rates) to install their existing facilities, and railway capital was only written off relatively recently. The words 'long-run marginal cost' ought to involve one in the cost of raising capital for replacement or expansion in the future, yet in practice current costs are held to include interest burdens inherited from the past. In fact the phrase 'bygones are bygones' is a little misleading, in that a company which failed to earn a modest rate of return on capital in the past would find its ability to raise capital in the future adversely affected.

It is plainly rather important to distinguish between *ex ante* and *ex post* margins, with the latter often a consequence of disparities between original plans or expectations and what is actually happening.

There are some interesting discussions about overheads, fixed and variable costs, avoidable and unavoidable expenditures. Useful as all this is, it tends to leave out one rather important aspect, of great significance for nationalised industries, that is, that these costs are *avoidable by whom*? If the post office can avoid delivering letters to remote areas (as is the case in some countries),[23] this transfers expenditures to someone else, in this case the customer, which may or may not be to the general advantage. A bus undertaking can avoid expenditure and not run a bus on a 'school' route, thereby imposing unavoidable (and perhaps on balance greater) net expenditure on the education authority. One might have thought that nationalisation would enable such matters to be considered. However, the institutional means for considering them are lacking, and economists might well have contributed to this by 'fragmented' thinking.

It is my contention that micro-economic theory, as commonly presented, incorrectly describes the way in which firms operate. In particular, margins, instead of being multi-level and having a context, become wrongly presented as if they are isolated and unconnected, on just one level. Therefore it is found possible to abstract from purpose, as if it was irrelevant, or even a non-economic category. This can cause serious error when applied to nationalised industries. I once tried to call the disease 'vulgarmarginalismus'. It could also be called 'purposeless marginalism'.

Let me, first of all, apply the concept 'purpose' to a firm in a competitive market. It studies the market. The firm may decide to go into the business of manufacturing cars, or providing restaurants. It chooses its purpose by reference to profitability, to the expected return on its investments. It must look carefully at the kind of cars or restaurants which it will supply; luxury, popular or intermediate categories. Having decided, it is then bound to undertake a complex of activities related to its chosen purpose. Some are absolutely necessary: cars must have four wheels and a spare; a kitchen must have frying pans. Others are not fixed in this way. *Filet mignon* need not always be on the menu, engines could be designed in a number of alternative ways, carburettors could be made by the firm or purchased from another manufacturer, and so on *ad infinitum*. However, all these decisions can only be taken rationally in relation to the defined objectives which the firm is pursuing. These objectives can, naturally, be redefined. The firm may decide to move from luxury cars to popular models, or out of luxury restaurants into hamburger bars. Then the needs and choices will be different.

Textbooks all too frequently omit to mention that the pursuit of the chosen (and profitable) purpose will very frequently lead the firms into actions which, save in the context of that purpose, could quite clearly be unprofitable. Ideally, if all things were infinitely divisible, mobile, non-specific, perhaps this would not happen. Then each stage and each decision would yield the same rate of return separately computed, and the shades of Pareto and Walras would be satisfied. However, we are dealing with a real world, and within it with a *theory of the firm*. As already stressed repeatedly, firms tend to be influenced, in their size and their organisation, by their ability to administer internally what otherwise would be externalities. Since it is an important part of their existence and *raison d'être*, it cannot be assumed away, not even in a theory of the firm. Yet organisational-institutional considerations have virtually been driven out of micro-economics.

Thus after-sales service, with stocks of parts readily available, could well appear to be an unprofitable tie-up of assets. Probably this is why in the USSR this is an outstandingly weak point. Stress on profitability (as distinct from plan fulfilment) would not of itself correct this, unless there is competition. There was even a (British) car firm which, possibly influenced by *vulgarmarginalismus*, decided that quality control was not worth while because it cost less to repair cars under guarantee after they went wrong! But this last case occurred in the competitive west, and the error was punished by very poor commercial results.

Similarly, the restaurant may decide to have a lavish menu, because a lavish menu pays, rather than because each item on it gives a rate of return of x per cent. The 'safari park' which announces 'open every day of the year' considers that *this* pays, though they do not make money every day of the year. The same is true with 24-hour garages. Because of indivisibilities, problems of peak demand, goodwill, even salesmanship (loss leaders, for instance), loss-making is often part of the pre-condition for profit-making.

But, as already pointed out, the attitude of the monopolist to peak demand can be quite different from that of the firm in a competitive market. Take electricity. Investments required for capacity used only at peak periods (in Britain this means very cold weather) will not pay as such. However, if consumers know that they will be switched off when it is very cold, they will install a different fuel. Consequently, a wise electricity company will certainly have the capacity to deal with peak demand (save perhaps in some rare and unusual circumstances). Britain's nationalised electricity industry must do this too, on commercial grounds, for it too 'suffers' from competition. However, suppose that there were no effective alternative. Then it would seem commercially quite sound to refrain from making investments in 'peak load' capacity. For indeed these additional investments would not pay. People would then suffer power cuts. If they objected, they could be told, 'Ah, you are asking us not to behave commercially, you are developing an economically unsound, social service concept.' To which one would reply, 'Nonsense, we are asking you to behave as a firm would have in fact behaved under competitive conditions.' To impose on a monopoly in these circumstances the duty to supply all customers on all normal occasions is a necessary substitute for competition.

Or put it another way. In a competitive market firms choose their role by reference to profitability. Their chosen role involves them in a complex of actions, which benefit consumers of goods and services. If a firm decides to cease to provide goods or a service, others can take its place. Duty or function need not be explicitly defined, not because they do not exist, but because the market does the defining. But a nationalised industry is in fact given a function to perform. It is protected from competition in order to perform it. Then its choices must be made by reference to this function. In some instances this is indeed recognised. Thus in Britain the gas undertaking must supply any customer. But this is not the rule, and some economists would say that statutory duty is anomalous and should be abandoned, along with similar obligations once imposed upon the railways.

This concept of imposed or contractual duty exists, unnoticed in the normal business of private firms, and is best seen in the category of franchise. Suppose a corporation (public or private, it makes no difference) signs a contract with a firm giving it sole rights to supply some goods or service. An example: catering at an airport. The firm operates upon negotiated conditions. These could include staying open 24 hours, serving a minimum number of hot dishes (perhaps at some maximum price) at all times, and so on. The firm, once it accepts these conditions, operates the franchise, which, as a whole, is profitable for it. If it ceases to be profitable, it can re-negotiate the terms. But it cannot claim to be acting 'efficiently' if, in the name of marginal analysis, it decides to serve no hot dishes between midnight and 6 a.m. on the grounds that to do so does not 'pay', because it has been granted its monopoly at the airport, its franchise, on conditions which include doing just that. This is exactly analogous to the 'Parliamentary train' decreed in 1844, referred to in Chapter 1.

Once again I envisage a critic saying, 'Yes, yes, but theories operate in an abstract and simplified world. Once the theorists deal with real things, they would naturally take reality into account. They are not prevented from doing so by the theory.'

To which the answer is, 'Alas, they seem to be, though perhaps they ought not to be'. To illustrate this, let us take an example which can be found in many textbooks, heard in lectures, read in answers to examination questions: investment criteria, with special reference to nationalised industries. We shall be discussing later in the paper the important and related issue of the rate of discount or interest-rate appropriate to nationalised industry. Here I have in mind a different aspect of the problem: how one determines what kind of investment to make. To what end is it made?

Textbook analysis is often ambiguous on this point. Is one discussing choice between alternative ways of achieving a given objective, or is one choosing the objective? Is one dealing with a competitive firm which provides goods or a service also provided by many other firms, or is one considering an industry or process as a whole? Is the investment 'self-contained', or is it part of a system or chain of activities? What, in an investment decision, are the decisive factors which must be taken into account?

On all this, all too often, the books are silent. Instead, students are taught a distinction (of some considerable importance, agreed) between ways of computing the financial results which flow from the investment: internal rates of return *versus* discounted cash flows (DCF). In some circumstances, we are told, they can yield different results, and it can be shown that DCF is the sounder of the two. In the Select Committee evidence already cited, economists and officials deplored the reluctance of some managers to use DCF, which is the officially approved method for British nationalised industries.

However, all this seems to me to leave the essential features of an investment decision out of account. In particular, the formal doctrine leaves undefined the vital question of how one decides what to do. It is implied that what needs doing is itself defined by and in the DCF calculation; many students and some teachers certainly think so.

In some circumstances they think rightly. Suppose that a firm under competition is contemplating an investment to increase the output of an imaginary commodity called widgets. It estimates what profits it would make, in relation to a particular magnitude of its investment project. At a given discount rate, it might well find that it paid to make more widgets, i.e. to invest in a bigger widget-making factory. If interest rates rise, the attractiveness of this investment might decline. The firm might build a smaller factory, it might in fact decide not to invest in widget-making at all. If it is to expand, the firm can do so in several ways, using alternative techniques. In this instance, it is indeed the case that not only the means but the end are variables. This form of presentation is therefore not wrong, though it does under-emphasise uncertainty about the future as a decisive factor.

However, all this becomes seriously misleading when one considers a nationalised industry such as electricity. We are here dealing with the whole industry, not with one unit. We are therefore concerned with total demand for electricity, and its evolution over time. Surely an input-output table plus foresight are of far greater importance here than DCF? What happens to demand for electricity is a function of the input requirements of electricity users. These could, of course, be affected by changes in relative costs, prices, productivity, and also by availability of alternative fuels. There might be a reduction in the tax on fuel oil, or a rise in the price of coal, and so on. So the input-output table would require modification, and a predominant role in the whole calculation would be played by the fact of uncertainty. If we make the right kind of guesses about the future intentions of electricity users, and about technical changes affecting fuels, then we can arrive at the demand for electricity in six years' time. It takes six years to design and build a power station. Much can happen in this time. We could be wrong. But if we are right, then it will surely be possible to charge an amount which will yield the required rate of profit. The latter would be the consequence of a correct estimation of the uncertainties, and, compared with the danger of wrong estimation, the difference between DCF and internal rate of return is a trivial matter.

The same point (as I found after I had written the above) was made by Kornai, using the same example. He contrasted a decision to increase the output of cloth by a few thousand metres next week with 'an electricity company deciding whether to create a new hydroelectric plant. The first decision is largely controlled by the market. In making the latter decision, however, it is not customary to reason that "the price of electricity has risen, so let us build a new power plant", or "the price of electricity has fallen, so there is no need for new investments in power plants". Instead, efforts are made to assess the future development and structure of the economy and to analyse the future demand for energy.'[24]

This applies to any major decision, in private corporations too. To cite a recent article, 'terrible disasters (like the Edsel) result from gross and elementary errors of concept, not from marginal mistakes in abstruse calculations like discounted cash flow. Yet intelligent men plump for one project rather than another on the strength of a difference of a few decimal points in the rate of return calculated over the next decade.'[25]

Far from trivial, of course, is the choice of how to meet a given future demand for electricity. There are choices to be made, between hydro and thermal, large and small, located at A or B, and so on. This could well be affected by the discount rate. But in what sense ought today's discount rate or prices to affect our estimation of the need for electricity in six years' time? If a competitive firm decides not to invest, it does not matter much; other firms also exist. But failure to provide enough power matters a great deal, as it is a vital input for many industries.

The same point emerges clearly if one contemplates an investment within a system of activities. In a sense the logic is the same. Just as an increase in the output of power-users requires more power to be provided, so the movement of more oil requires more tankers, or pipelines, industrial development in a new area requires housing, and so on. Trivial? No, because it underlines two things. The first is that the profitability of the complementary activity has to be judged in some relation with what it is complementary to. The failure to provide tankers, houses, etc, affects the profits of other undertakings, and consequently this is relevant to the investment decisions under consideration. Secondly, it underlines the importance, in such cases, of clarity on how far the objective is given: often (not always) the investment decision concerns not *what* but *how*. Thus tankers or houses could be built and operated by the corporation, by separate firms, and they could be of many different kinds; but they have to be built.

This is not for a moment to deny that there are other cases,

57

also involving nationalised industries, in which one has to decide whether or not to undertake some activity. My object was simply to stress that an important distinction is blurred by an analysis which concentrated on cash flows and neglected purpose.

Another way of illustrating the essence of the problem is to think for a moment of the relationship between a large firm and one of its many sub-contractors. The large firm decides what needs to be done and makes it worth the sub-contractors' while to do it. It must be noted that neither the decision about what to do, nor the principal's evaluation of the efficiency with which it is done, depends upon the profit-and-loss account of the sub-contractor. If the task for which the sub-contractor is employed were to be undertaken by a sub-unit owned by the firm itself, the same logic applies.

Chapter 3

The Argument applied to
Eastern Europe

All this, if accepted, has a considerable bearing on the reform discussion of East European countries. Profitability can often appear different at different levels of decision-making, because at each level the decision-maker internalises more (takes more interrelationships into account). It follows that the level at which decisions are taken affects resource allocation. This is in fact true whatever the criterion of efficiency chosen, whether it is gross value of output, sales, labour productivity or profit. In the USSR under Stalin, as under capitalism, a manager of a paper-mill would find it pays him to pollute a river, unless stopped by some superior authority which has an interest also in fish. Much of the discussion on the role of profit in managerial decisions in the east seems to ignore these matters. It is often blithely assumed that rationality equals decentralisation, via profits and prices, to the firm or enterprise (in the USSR this is usually a factory or plant). Yet a manager of a factory producing soda ash in the USSR has an analogous position to the manager of just such a factory within I.C.I. Why should the Russian have more power to respond to profit, as he conceives and perceives it, than his British opposite number? The whole question of decentralisation, in the USSR or in a western corporation, is complex, and raises all the questions we have been discussing here. How odd that, in an age of great corporations, the 'theory of the firm' should have so little to say about them. In fact very few economists have considered it worth while to inquire how a corporation organises its affairs. When, over ten years ago, I was writing my book on the Soviet economy, I wrote in the introduction that it was odd that so

59

few economists had inquired as to how that economy works. I showed my draft to an eminent colleague at the London School of Economics, where I was then teaching. The colleague commented, 'But hardly anyone inquires how our economy works'. It is not quite as true as it was in 1960, but almost.

But to return to Eastern Europe. Their problem was the opposite one. Under Stalin they claimed that they could 'internalise' everything, that they were able to substitute the interest of the whole national economy, indeed of society, for the profitability of a part. Unfortunately, this is not possible. 'Internalisation' on such a scale is not only exceedingly costly, in terms of collection and processing of information about means and ends; it is self-defeating. To organise 'centralised' management of the whole economy, it is necessary to create a complex bureaucracy which is perforce divided into parts or ministries. These have usually been based on sectors (metallurgy, heavy engineering, coal, chemicals, textiles, retail trade, and so on), and then further sub-divided down to the level of enterprise director. True, they are all subject to 'the plan', which is drafted by a coordinating agency (Gosplan) and is binding on everybody. However, highly imperfect information about what is needed, the necessity to aggregate in order to deal with manageable numbers, the reliance on reports and proposals from below, and the unavoidable bureaucratisation, produce a whole number of diseconomies of scale familiar to the student of the Soviet economy, and which it is unnecessary to go into here in detail. Ministries disaggregate global output targets and instruct 'their' enterprise managers to fulfil plans expressed in tons, or roubles, or metres, or some other unit of measurement. These plans are a function partly of information about requirements of users (unavoidably aggregated, as in full detail the number of variables becomes unmanageably large), partly of indents and proposals received from management. The importance of the upward flow of information and of proposals is so great that one Eastern economist commented, 'You should not call our system a command economy because so many commands are written by their recipients.' The link between customer and supplier is weak, partly because of the vertical nature of lines

60

of hierarchical subordination, partly owing to the chronic sellers' market situation. No doubt one could conceive of a superplanner who 'internalises' all the information in the context of an all-inclusive social welfare function. Unfortunately, there is not and cannot be such a superplanner (or function). Some fragmentation, decentralisation, devolution, is inescapable. Equally inescapable, therefore, are the problems with which we have been concerned, and which admit of no easy solution, under 'centralised' planning or under capitalism.

The essential point is that for each enterprise and ministerial division the rest of the economy is an 'externality'. This affects their behaviour in proposing plans, and in executing aggregated plans (e.g. making metal goods as heavy as possible to fulfil plans in tons). Told to keep costs down, they frequently try to do so at the expense of their customers, whether these be another state enterprise or a consumer. It is no use appealing to a 'socialist spirit' or the common good, because the common good is supposed to be embodied in the output and cost reduction plans and is not otherwise readily identifiable. In practice, as critics of the Stalin model have been pointing out, the absence of a market and price mechanism deprives the planners of vital information about both what is needed and how it can be most economically provided.

Weaknesses such as these led to demands for the restoration of some species of market mechanism, at least for current decision-making and minor investments, such as would permit production to be based more directly upon consumer-producer (supplier) relationships, with a wide range of decentralised decision-making based upon price-and-profit computation. Many of the reformers, however, took pains to point out that investment decisions or technical advances of a major kind, which radically altered scarcity relationships and were in no sense marginal, required a different approach.

While reforms of a market-socialist species have made hardly any headway in the USSR, they have been firmly established in Yugoslavia and, in a less far-reaching form, also in Hungary.

In these countries inevitably, the problems we have been

61

discussing here are bound to be raised. Indeed, they have arisen in the USSR also, in so far as profitability (subject to plan fulfilment) is now an important bonus-creating indicator, and it was soon observed that profits under monopoly can be increased at the cost of the customer's time and convenience. In the USSR the necessity or desirability of competition is denied. In Yugoslavia and Hungary it is accepted and encouraged. But this, while representing in some sectors an unquestionable improvement over bureaucratic centralism, leaves a number of problems unsolved.

Confining our attention to production rather than to strategic investment decisions, we can perhaps best tackle these issues by looking briefly at the prewar Lange model of socialism. Lange, let us recall, saw the possibility of a species of socialist *tâtonnement*. The centre could fix prices, which eventually represent a balance between supply and demand; the managers would follow the marginal-revenue-equals-marginal-cost rule, and efficiency would be attained. There are a number of questions that arise, some of them not very relevant to our present discussion, though important for the micro-economics of socialism. Thus how can a central planning board fix prices for a great multitude (literally millions) of products? What motive have all those concerned to act in accordance with Lange's rules? Moreover, as readers will surely have already observed, an important element of ambiguity is involved in the marginal cost rule, under socialism as under capitalism. Lange was, of course, engaged in the task of answering Robbins and Mises, and similar critics who urged that socialism could not be efficient. Lange sought to demonstrate that it could, and he did so at a level of unreality no greater than that used in the competitive or Walras-Paretian model. But this does not mean that a real socialist system could operate the Lange model without major qualifications and modifications.

At this point again I found myself at one with Janos Kornai, who has also argued that the Lange model is based on the same basic assumptions as the Walrasian general-equilibrium system. In particular, the only operational information required in the model was to be contained in prices, and the administrative-institutional complications (not to mention uncertainty, risk, inertia, routine, etc) were assumed out of the way. Of course, all this rests on an artificial base, which has only a remote relation to the real world under any system.

These qualifications are forgotten all too easily by both sides in the controversy. Thus I once attended a symposium at Ann Arbor at which the superior efficiency of capitalism was demonstrated as follows. The discussant drew a simple 'production possibilities frontier' diagram on the blackboard.

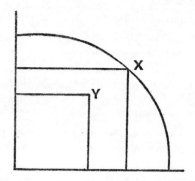

He then imagined that an entrepreneur under capitalism would pick a point (say x) on this frontier, since he knew what his production possibilities were. A Soviet type planner, however, would suffer from imperfect vision because of the hierarchical, multi-tier nature of the decision-making process. Consequently he would land up somewhere inside the frontier (say y).

Really! ! First of all, it is conceivable that the same entrepreneur under capitalism is misinformed, if not about his own production possibilities then about demand, or the latest technique, or something. But secondly and most important of all. the economist who made the above comparison is obviously mesmerised by the textbook entrepreneur, and seems unaware of great corporations with complex multi-tier bureaucracies. Some of these corporations have a turnover equal to that of a medium-sized socialist country. As already remarked, the manager of a factory within a corporation, say ICI at Grange-mouth, Scotland, may know his own production possibilities intimately, but his actions are still greatly circumscribed by a divisional manager, above whom is the Board of Directors in London. It is possible that they are aware of possibilities (and consequences) invisible at Grangemouth. Were it otherwise, full decentralisation to Grangemouth would be economically rational. London is far from Grangemouth, and, like any Soviet industrial ministry, headquarters would see some things less clearly than the manager on the spot. But, of course, anyone can commit an error, in any system.

The whole question of optimal organisation is intimately bound up with the identification of organisational economies and diseconomies of scale, of the internationalisation of externalities, of the cost of internalisation, the necessity of some degree of decentralisation—and of centralisation too. It is no simple matter, to be dealt with by artificial 'one-dimensional' diagrams. If the western system does work more efficiently, it is not because it differs from the Soviet or Roumanian one by having no hierarchies with men remote at the top whose vision is imperfect. (What, one may ask, of the international company?).

Nor can such problems be dealt with by naive 'Libermanism', after that worthy but over-rated Soviet industrial economist. 'Whatever is advantageous for society should be profitable for the enterprise.' So it should be, were there no such things as those we have been discussing throughout these pages. A Soviet 'enterprise' is a factory or plant. Is the profit of ICI Grangemouth necessarily consistent with that of ICI? If not, why should the profit of its Soviet equivalent necessarily be consistent with that of its own Ministry of Chemical industry?

Libermanism becomes no more practicable if it is given mathematical expression. One hears in the east of 'parametric prices', these having the function of relating local optima to the overall optimum, so that the pursuit of micro-profitability would lead to the national optimum. Unfortunately, life is more complicated than that.

'It is obvious that the concept of an economy controlled by shadow prices (computed from a linear programming model, A.N.) is related to the G(eneral) E(quilibrium) school. It is built

64

on the same basic assumptions: optimisation, preference ordering, exclusiveness of price information. . . .'[26] Kornai again, hitting the nail on the head. At this point a theoretical excursus is called for. Those uninterested in theory can skip the next paragraphs, though this would be a pity.

First a word on shadow prices. These are not actual prices, but those which are corrected to take into account some distorting factors operating today or, more relevant to planning and investment, the state of affairs which will exist in the future. Thus if there is a surplus of electricity generation capacity, or pigs, or steel today, prices should fall. But if correct foresight enables one to predict, with or without the help of a computer programme, that there will be shortages tomorrow if this price were maintained, then decisions relating to tomorrow should use higher shadow prices. A long-term plan, computerised in a linear programme, would have as its 'dual' (i.e. as its logical reflection) a set of prices which are by definition optimal shadow prices. They would orientate all subordinate units, each of them maximising its own profits, towards fulfilling the plan. The plan, in turn, would be optimal, in that, with given resources, it would be computed to maximise the welfare function of society or of the planners.

Alas, this is a mistaken approach on a number of counts. First of all, planners have no operationally usable set of preferences.[27] It is an absurd thing to use the wishes of the supreme political authority as the criterion of optimality. A Soviet mathematical economist once told me, 'The political leadership turns to us for advice as to what they should do. If we tell them that what they wish is our criterion of the efficacy of the system, they would tell us to go to hell, and they would be right.' Kornai made the same point succinctly; 'It is empty advice to recommend that the decision-maker maximise his own utility function. It reminds us of a popular saying in Budapest; "If you want my opinion, you should do as you please".'[28] Similarly, the social welfare function is an imaginative piece of fiction, never identified in reality because it is never identifiable. So *what* is one optimising?

Secondly, to compute a shadow price you require information.

But the future is uncertain, and the uncertainty relates to many matters other than prices. This is another way of restating the point already made that price information, though always important, is only one element in decision-making, particularly if investment is involved.

Thirdly, as with the Lange model, this approach abstracts from institutions, patterns of human behaviour, inertia, routine, etc. It is nowhere explained why any of the economic actors should act, even if they do have information. Also, where are organisational economies of scale, external and internal economies, and all the problems attendant upon decentralisation?

Fourthly, in the long or even the medium run many of the 'constraints' are variables, because they can be altered by the investments which one could make if one chose.

Finally, what exactly *is* an optimum? What *is* the production possibilities frontier? How could one identify it, outside a textbook of economics? Quantification is desirable, of course. When the needed statistics are not available, they should be sought. But all we can ever know is what has occurred, not what could have occurred. Is the output of cars or widgets within this frontier in Ruritania? In one sense 'Yes', because it is impossible to conceive a situation which cannot be improved. It is the same for human beings. I *could* write better, and if I did not go to climb Ben Lomond tomorrow, or let myself be distracted by this very pretty girl, my output could perhaps be higher. Or is my propensity to climb hills or be distracted by girls 'parameters' or 'constraints', within which I optimise? Terms incapable of precise definition, purporting to express something which cannot either be quantified or tested against experience, should be used sparingly.

The real answer to the question, rightly put by students of comparative economic systems, about relative efficiency may well lie in a combination of competition and diversity of organisational forms. Competition in the western private sector usually either exists or could exist; even well-established dominant firms (e.g. Tate and Lyle in the sugar industry, or ICI in Britain, or IBM in the United States) are dominant on condition they are reasonably efficient, and they know it. Whereas, as a sad Czech economist once told me, 'There is nothing so monopolistic as a socialist monopoly.' The socialist Soviet-type 'firms' cannot compete among themselves, owing to the administrative allocation of their products, and they cannot choose their suppliers, for these too are (as a rule) designated by the planners. As for diversity, all Soviet enterprises are organised in a similar way, are subject to the same regulations, none of them are independent in the sense of being free to respond to profitable opportunities which they perceive, without first obtaining permission and resources from planners. There were cooperative artisans who would do this, within limits, but in the USSR at least they were abolished (as recently as 1961). Today, it is true, some experimentation is in progress, but this is in the direction of trusts and amalgamations. In contrast, large firms in the west vary in their internal arrangements (especially with regard to decentralisation), and there are very many quite small firms which can be fairly easily started and which can supply needs (including the needs of the giants, as sub-contractors) as and when they arise.

It may be of interest to illustrate the above analysis with a reference to the complementarity-indivisibility problem as it is seen in the USSR, in relation to investment criteria. This will have the merit both of highlighting the issue and showing up the limits of centralised 'internalisation'. The context was a conference held at Novosibirsk in 1971 on the subject of 'Planning multi-sector long-term investment programmes'.

The director of the Institute of Economics and Production Organisation at Novosibirsk, A. G. Aganbegyan, urged the adoption of a 'system approach'. This he defined as follows: 'Systems analysis consists above all in considering even the most remote aspects of the process under study in their interrelationships as elements of a single system. The system itself is set up from the standpoint of given aims and objectives. The elements of the system are interlinked and, taken together, they all carry out interrelated tasks. Further, every system is part of a wider system, it has defined "entrances" and "exits" ["inputs" and "outputs", perhaps? A. N.] It is necessary to work out

67

management parameters, which govern the development of the particular process under consideration. The identification of these parameters is essential, if we are considering economic systems, in order to set up the organisational structures of control of the system. If one examines a major long-term investment programme from the systems standpoint, it becomes clear that *construction work must be looked at not from the standpoint of its own efficiency (effektivnost'), of its own programme, but from the standpoint of total efficiency in the context of those projects which are being constructed on the basis of the given* [investment] *programme.* . . . Unfortunately this elementary principle . . . is by no means always observed.'[29]

Here Aganbegyan is arguing, as we have been urging, that actions which occur within systems of activities be assessed by reference to the system in which they occur. Why does he have to do this in the USSR, where, after all, no serious economic reform has occurred and in which centralised planning ought to take care of just such problems as these? He himself provides the answer. 'The second requirement of systems analysis consists in examining not each [investment] item separately, but a group of interlinked multi-sector objectives. *The investment programme must ensure the synchronised and balanced completion of projects. Often this does not happen, especially in Siberia, in considering large economic complexes, because, as a rule, each project belongs to its own department.*'[30] He gives the example of the completion of a great power station, the responsibility of the Ministry of Electric Power. However, the aluminium factory which should have used its power is very far behind schedule, which was lucky because the organs responsible for the bauxite would have failed to provide this necessary material. A colleague of his, V. Krasovski, refers to a timber complex which is the 'responsibility' of eight different departments or ministries, which overlap, fail to interrelate, and so on. 'Therefore departmental demarcation lines, the absence of complex interdepartmental construction programmes, of complex regional plans, is a cause of serious losses in the implementation of large-scale investment projects.'[31] The proposed solution is to create a regional project-management structure which would cut across ministerial-departmental lines.

The distortions about which Aganbegyan and his colleagues complain could arise because profitability of the parts fails to match the needs of the system, and we have seen that this could certainly happen. In the USSR profitability is not a dominant criterion, so the reasons would be different, related to administrative responsibility and priorities, in the context of plan fulfilment. Thus enterprise A, whose work is part of a complex investment project, has to carry out a plan made by its ministry, and is rewarded for doing so. The ministry's priorities and policies relate to the ministry's overall success indicators, and so enterprise A's plan may not conform to the requirements of the complex project. The measurement of plan fulfilment (e.g. in tons of output, value of work done, or whatever) would only coincidentally influence the manager of enterprise A to do just what is wanted for the project at the time at which it is wanted. The point is, as the Soviet discussion put it, that 'the aim of the development of the complex is not the maximisation of the function of each of the elements of which it is composed'.[32]

The observant reader will note that Aganbegyan's argument is not unlike the one adduced by William G. Shepherd, cited earlier ('decentralisation on a private-market model would yield an efficient solution at each unit only by a very remote chance'). True, Aganbegyan is not discussing a market, but both are pointing the dangers of sub-optimisation within a system of activities. Kornai is also aware of the problem, because he insists on the importance of systems analysis. Within a system, and consequential upon what he calls a 'fundamental' decision, various actions *must* follow, and in an order largely predetermined by the basic decision already taken. '. . . There are non-continuous response functions belonging to the non-continuous variables. "We can implement the first action only if we simultaneously begin the second one: . . . the third action is impossible since the fourth is already in process and these two exclude each other".'[33]

Therefore, in the USSR as elsewhere, the organisational

structure affects the kinds of decisions that are taken, and consciousness that this is so ought to penetrate the rarified world of micro-economic theory, there and here. It is perhaps instructive to note that coordination of activities under separate ownership and management through the market is sometimes easier to achieve than coordination of separate administrative agencies, such as ministries, because the latter cannot market their externalities. Nonetheless, as we have seen, in the west too the answer is sometimes found in a common management structure. This is one reason why firms are big.

In management and administration these ideas are by now reasonably familiar. A paper on my desk contains headings such as 'The hierarchy of networks', and 'The interrelationship of activities'. The problem is to link this sort of thing with economic theory.[34]

So I am far from arguing for the proposition that centralised socialist planning is able to cope better with the problems set by optimisation in a real world. Indeed, there is a strong case for saying that they do this badly. But we really must compare like with like, reality with reality, with all its imperfections. On the level of pure models, perfect planning and perfect competition are alike in being perfect.

Chapter 4

The Relation of Theory to Practice

A senior official of a large western corporation once said in a lecture, 'It takes young economists whom we employ a few months to forget about marginal cost pricing. Then we can start using them.' (He might have said, 'Forget about formal micro-economics'.) What did he mean by this?

If I understood him correctly, he had in mind two things. One, which happened to be important in his firm, was the introduction of new products. This necessarily involves risk, and even a successful innovation faces losses in the first year, when lack of experience causes running costs to be high, and yet the product cannot be launched at a full-cost-plus price, for then no one would buy it. This hopefully is followed by a period of much lower cost and an above-average profit, which lasts until the competitors have caught on and force the price down, say three years later.

Secondly, like all modern industry, this one has very high fixed costs. Consequently marginal costs tend to be below average costs until capacity is fully utilised, and further production requires substantial new investments (substantial owing to indivisibilities, economies of scale, etc.), whereupon the process is repeated, so the cost curve might look like this:

What are marginal costs? Bearing in mind the customers' dislike of frequent and unpredictable price changes, the company hopefully uses average costs as the basis. Is it wrong to do so?

Conventional theory is, of course, aware of increasing returns. However, as already indicated, it tends to treat them as an exception, or as a kind of early stage in a cost curve which turns decisively upwards in due course, and not as a recurring phenomenon which is encountered whenever a corporation or product reaches full production and instals new capacity. Needless to say, this does not 'dispose' of marginal analysis, since it must exist whenever marginal decisions are taken. But seeking the advantage of the whole firm, in a fluid situation in which there are many interdependencies through time, requires the corporation executive to see each decision in terms of the corporation's long-term profits, not solely in terms of the revenue related to the particular costs which are the subject of analysis. This seems obvious enough, yet one lecturer on nationalised industries could and did assert that the require-ment to show an overall rate of profit was irrational; what was rational was the conformity of each part or decision (e.g. investment decision) to the DCF rule.

Let us, then, look again at theory. What ought it to do? First, in my view, it requires to look again at the theory of the firm, a theory which should have some bearing on real firms. At quite an early stage the student could be introduced to the significance of organisation and its relation to decision-making. While no doubt he could be told that there exist conglomerates in which the separate units engage in totally unrelated activi-ties, he could be told that a firm is a system of activities and units which are linked together, not only by a common manage-ment structure but also by a degree of indivisibility and inter-dependency, some to do with processes of production or distribution, some with goodwill, often with both. This line of thought finds some reflection in the now fashionable 'Manage-ment by objective', but this is no part of micro-theory.

In many courses the element of system within micro-econ-omics is introduced as a species of exception. Thus electricity generation is an interlinked system physically, and so the student is told (if he is told anything as practical as this) that costs are system costs and revenues are system revenues. He is seldom told that this is no exception, but merely a particularly striking and evident instance of the general rule.

All this would be easier if micro-economic theory were

expanded to take an interest in industries, or sectors, rather than only in individuals or firms of indeterminate size. (For most of the theory, as we have seen, they must be small enough to fit into the competitive or Paretian model.) Macro-economics deals with much larger aggregates, such as GNP, or global savings or investments. In between lies a vast no-man's land which theory only occasionally examines. Economists do, naturally, discuss specific problems relating to an industry. Steel, electricity, textiles, rail or road transport, have been written about, investigated, analysed. However, this is most often and most fruitfully accomplished by 'applied economists', concerned with practice and not with theory at all. It has often been remarked that there is a gap between the 'theory' and 'applied' parts of many an economics course, and this is so indeed. But there is also a gap between micro-economic theory (and theorists) and the problems of large units or segments, situated between the firm and macro-economic aggregates. So when the theorist does pay attention to a large segment of the economy, as he must do when he deals with a nationalised industry, he instinctively applies the ideas which make sense in an uncoordinated (or rather market-coordinated) world of small administratively unrelated units.

The more the theorists' attention can be directed to large scale and industry-wide affairs, the more he must be aware (and make his student aware) of links, systems, internalities and the like. These ideas are not difficult for even a first year student to grasp. They will not teach anyone to resolve the actual problems of the steel, railway or any other industry. But they will at least help—and not hinder—those who tackle these problems when they study, as they must, the 'specifics' of the given sector.

If one's attention is diverted from typical micro (and fragmented) thinking to an industry, say the steel (or pin) industry, then the notion of purpose can become that much clearer. The object of an industry is not primarily to do with marginal revenue or marginal cost; it exists to provide steel and pins respectively. In the 'perfect-competitive' model this need not be said explicitly, not because it is not true, but because the behaviour of the infinite number of steel or pin producers is not affected by any explicit purpose. Steel or pins are provided through the autonomous profit-seeking behaviour of the firms, any of which is free at any time to move to some other line of business. We have already noted the necessity to analyse the logic of a firm's chosen role, even under competition. But this does not affect the validity of the proposition that the firm, pursuing its profits[35] in a perfect market will provide what needs to be provided. (Of course, the steel or other industry's size, output, investment, will be, must be, affected by conventional micro-economic criteria, to an extent which we will be discussing later). But an industry-wide analysis would take the provision of goods and services by that industry for granted as its purpose, and evidently will continue to do so when and if the industry becomes nationalised. This would save us from some elementary distortions. So would the incorporation of a little input-output logic. To produce A one must have B, C, perhaps D, and either E or F. Iron ore is produced because it is essential for iron and steel. The profitability is derived from this necessity. Of course this is a statement of the obvious. But sometimes students' eyes are kept firmly and exclusively to increments, margins and profitability, so that the object of the exercise is lost from view.

This brings me to the major issue of the correct presentation of margins and increments. A little time really should be spent on defining what margins are, and to saying that the meaning of the word, or rather its applicability in practice to a defined 'product', is far from self-evident. There is also much to be said for introducing the concept of multi-dimensional margins and linking it with the structure of the firm or of an industry. There is the marginal pair of shoes, the marginal batch of shoes of a given design and quality, or the marginal decision concerning all shoes of that design and quality, the marginal factory, shoe shop, group of shoe shops, stocks kept by wholesale traders in footwear, etc. Just so there is a marginal goods wagon, goods train, siding, service, branch, line, peak-load services on the line, and so on. Some of these things are connected (e.g. sales, stocks and production of footwear), some are parts of a larger whole (e.g. a batch of shoes or a type of shoes within the output

74

of a factory, or a train on a line). In these instances, and in many others one could quote, decisions about the various margins are unlikely to be taken at the same level by the same person. One can imagine, alongside margins within other margins, an organisational diagram in which various officials of the corporation are taking decisions. When a 'marginal' decision at a given level has insignificant 'internal' effects on the rest of the firm, the power to act can be devolved to the relatively junior official or manager at that level, since centralisation always involves some cost. Thus managers can be authorised to buy furniture for their offices, and a stationmaster can arrange his station's litter disposal. However, other decisions would involve information, action, effects on profitability, which cannot be adequately assessed at the level of this employee, sector, branch or whatever. Hence the need for rules about who decides what in any corporation, and hence a hierarchy within which certain defined questions, or expenditures involving sums exceeding a given amount, have to be referred to headquarters. Within headquarters too, some matters can be settled at junior-official level, others have to go to the managing director or the board. Bureaucracy is not only a governmental phenomenon. Within a corporation bureaucracy, as in a civil service, one must consider (*inter alia*) precedent, i.e. the fact that one decision may logically involve another one at a future date in an analogous situation (though in business this is less binding than in a civil service, it exists in all large organisations, even in universities).[36] This should remind one that conservatism and inertia are common faults in human affairs, and economic organisations are by no means free of them, unless competition, or some substitute for competition, supplies a strong prod. And even then. . . . One is reminded of an interesting controversy, which has brought life to a segment of micro-economics, that of motivation of corporation executives: the concept of 'satisficing' as distinct from maximising.

The concept of 'satisficing' has given rise to widespread controversy. It can be derived from studies of corporation bureaucracies, with their interdepartmental conflicts and compromises, and the separation of management from owner-

ship. If one accepts this hypothesis, then after all the management of nationalised industries is asked to behave no differently
from corporation executives in aiming for some rough average
profitability target. However, the maximising hypothesis
happens to be convenient for formal theory and it has many
defenders. For reasons already examined, it cannot be tested,
since all we know is what occurred, not the most which could
have occurred, and it seems trivial or futile to equate the actual
with the best possible outcome.

There is a hierarchy of margins, broadly analogous to
hierarchy of organisation and to some extent explaining the
existence of the latter. (There are other reasons too, no doubt:
technological economies of scale and purely informational
problems, for instance). A given transaction, an investment
decision, a service, even a dish on a restaurant menu, may or
may not pay, but even though each may involve an identifiable
cost and revenue, the correct decision would depend in some
degree on the context, on the 'location' of the marginal decision
under consideration within the totality of the activities of the
corporation. 'Location' is used deliberately, as it is a term
which could apply both to where the *margin* is situated in the
production activities of the corporation, and where the *decision*
is situated in the administrative set-up.

A 'margin' does not cease to be part of a related whole if the
economic activity with which it is concerned is part of a separate
purchase-and-sale transaction and has its own price. This,
though elementary, is often missed. Separate charging is
frequently a matter of convention. A cup of tea includes sugar
in most countries, but until recently in the USSR there was an
extra charge, in popular cafés at least. In most countries the use
of a w.c. on a train or plane is free, but at a station or terminal
one must pay, a fact which led British Rail actually to close
some small-station w.cs, as they did not pay! A car park by a
supermarket is conventionally free, a car park by a station is
not. Yet these 'parts' do not cease to be part of the same
complex, with obvious 'internal effects', merely because
separately charged for. British Rail recently increased by
50–100 per cent the charges they make for car parking at

stations in London suburbs. 'Frankly we are charging what the market will bear,' explained a spokesman. Remarkable concept for a nationalised industry, and if this same man were running a supermarket everyone would know he needed his head examining. Yet this aim to maximise revenue from car parks *qua* car parks is apparently regarded as sound economics. My imaginary course on micro-economics would use this as an elementary example of muddled fragmentation-thinking. Station car parks should then be 'hived off' to private companies. Why not, on this logic?

I have heard cross-subsidisation criticised, yet the critics seemed to have no answer to the following two examples, which I would also bring into elementary micro-economics. One I used in my *Economic Journal* article, and apologise for its re-use. Imagine two small private airlines, one of which flies from A to B, the other from B to C. Some passengers change planes at B and proceed to C. The first airline proposes to alter its flights so that the connection will not any longer be made. Let us say it loses £1000 net compared with using this aircraft on another route. Let us suppose that the second airline would lose £3000 as a result of the change. What would happen? Communications would be established, and if the second airline were to pay £1500 to the first, both would be better off than they would have been if the service were abandoned. This elementary instance of the marketing of externalities would be institutionally impracticable within a large corporation (state or private). Thus the man in charge of route A to B has no right to pay his colleague who runs route B to C to persuade him to continue or to inaugurate a service. This is headquarters business. At headquarters they may take economic orthodoxy seriously. Each part must pay, each line must be regarded as a profit-making sub-unit, following the ideas of Munby and his numerous colleagues. To use the profits on one part to cover the losses in another is the very definition of cross-subsidisation. So the men at headquarters would pause, and perhaps consult economic advisers. They may say, 'Cross-subsidisation is irrational'. Payment of a loss of one line out of the profits of another is cross-subsidisation. Therefore it is irrational.

Were they to argue so, they would provide a good case for Mises-like criticism of public enterprise. For two small airlines would, by marketing their externalities, achieve an economically better result than a state corporation which, through misunderstanding economic doctrine, resolutely externalises its internalities. I say 'misunderstanding' because, properly interpreted, orthodox doctrine should not apply the term 'cross-subsidisation' to situations bristling with indivisibilities and complementarities. Unfortunately, the sort of point just made seldom finds a place in textbooks or teaching, and so the misunderstanding, when it occurs, is the responsibility of the profession.

My second example is a bridge or tunnel. Its construction may cost, let us say, £5 million. It may add £40 million to property values. This would make the project profitable for society if there were a toll of zero. The analogy with the supermarket's car park suggests itself. True, in the latter case the users tend to spend money in the supermarket, whereas the beneficiaries of the tunnel or bridge are many and may escape making any contribution to its cost. This sets up problems about the best way to pay for the project. Many ideas exist: a levy on property values, or the purchase by the authority of land in the area and its subsequent resale, or, of course, a toll. So long as there is no toll, no one can compute the separate profitability of the bridge or tunnel, and cost-benefit analysis comes naturally in respect of the project as a whole. But a toll at once sets some minds going in computing the return on the bridge, and the transfer to the accounts, to cover 'losses on the bridge', and profit in real estate can look yet again like cross-subsidisation.

Far-fetched? No, we have already quoted many examples in similar logical categories. It leads, among other things, to the 'hiving off' philosophy of the Conservatives. Why should BEA be in the hotel and package tour business, and why should British Rail run hotels? They should make their profits out of their basic tasks. As if American railroads in their heyday did not make the bulk of their profits out of land values!

If the large-scale enterprise or the corporation has been emphasised in these last few pages, it is mainly because it gives organisational reflection to the 'multi-dimensional marginalism' advocated here. But in fact the same principles can be identified as operating within the mind of a small businessman. For instance, the small shopkeeper in the Scottish village where these lines are being written decides what to stock, not only in terms of the turnover figures for jam, plates, ham and dates. He also considers what kind of shop his customers expect, and whether too small a selection will cause them to travel to the nearest town, where, of course, they will also be able to get the kind of goods which are particularly profitable for him to stock. In this case, the multiple levels are not in a hierarchy of employees but in his own head. The economic reality is the same.

This brings one to the concept of chosen role and its logic. Since this is an accurate description of reality, including competitive reality, there is no reason why this should not be said in textbooks and lectures. Quite plainly economic men, managers and entrepreneurs choose their role and this involves them in a set of acts which occur within it and are meaningful within it. This is true of human behaviour in general. We do not always do what we would prefer to do. Thus I have chosen the role of university teacher, and therefore must sometimes give lectures on matters about which I would prefer not to lecture yet again, and read dull examinations scripts which, were I engaged in some different profession, I would certainly refuse to read. I have room for manoeuvre and try to avoid reading too many scripts, but a minimum is inescapable. So too a firm which chooses to promise regular deliveries to its customers must sometimes keep its promise at times when it is financially inconvenient to itself. Obvious? Yet our textbook marginal analysis is philosophically analogous to the proposition that no one performs any act which, in terms of his preferences, he prefers not to perform. Presented in such one-dimensional language, it would follow that I should not correct examination scripts, and a firm should not take any decision which does not yield some minimum rate of return. Of course, if challenged, the textbook's author would demur, 'I meant to take the whole situation into account, naturally'. Logically this is what he ought to have meant, even perhaps what he did mean. Unfortunately he seldom bothers to say so.

So, at the cost of labouring what ought to be obvious, firms and entrepreneurs choose roles, or a function, one which seems to them likely to 'pay'. This involves them in a complex of acts, some avoidable, some (within this role) unavoidable. The role itself is re-definable, modifiable, even avoidable in total (one can sell out and do something else). Whatever else is chosen will carry with it its own associated complex of activities. Theory should distinguish between those aspects of the complex which are part of the productive process (e.g. tightening up nuts and bolts on a car assembly line, or making beds in a hotel), and those related or complementary activities which are detachable, are separately priced and may be conducted by other firms (e.g. after-sales service for cars, transport to a hotel, and so on). It is obvious and indeed trivial to insist that cars must have wheels and hotels have beds. It is all included in the price anyway. It is when some set of transactions affects other transactions that the difficulty arises and theory tends to be silent, and theorists tend to offer misleading advice.

It might also be useful for theorists who write about investment criteria to do so with some attention to the object that the investment is intended to fulfil, or the goods or service which it is intended to provide. Here a narrowly conceived marginalism does particularly obvious harm. Under perfect competition with perfect divisibility, an investment provides an increment or something. With a given price, and a rate of interest of x per cent, investments will tend to an equilibrium position at which the rate of return (conceived as DCF if this is preferred) will be equal whatever it is and wherever this increment is located in the national economy. If, then, in a particular sector the rate of return is above this figure, then investments will be made until the rate is brought down to it; if it is below then, naturally, no investment will be made. In a one-dimensional economy this all sounds logical enough. But then it is applied to individual investment in nationalised industries, and one hears repeatedly that the use of DCF for these purposes is somehow superior to the more naive practice in current use in private industry. Even elementary textbooks could draw attention to the fallacies or errors which follow from such an unimaginative application of theory.

Let us accept that a completely integrated industry with above-average profitability should attract more investment. In this sense, assuming increasing marginal costs, it is indeed the case that investments should be such as would bring the firm to a level of output at which marginal revenue equals marginal costs, and this would be the level at which the rate of return would equal the cut-off point set by the prevailing discount rate, leaving net profits of zero over and above this rate. These considerations would therefore determine the magnitude of the investment. In the real world this would all be modified by uncertainty, errors caused by imperfect information, and also by the uneven impact of technical progress. This would be accepted by all economists: one cannot accurately predict the unpredictable, though one must do one's best. Obviously investment decisions will represent estimates of the future situation. This only enters into the present argument in so far as the availability of information, the ability to predict, may determine the locations of investment decisions within a corporation hierarchy. The point to be stressed here is a different one. It is that in the real world, even assuming away the element of uncertainty, most investment choices are made in a context in which the size and nature of the project is *not* determined by its rate of return, because the investment decision will very frequently be a part of a larger whole, integrated within it to a greater or lesser degree, and the more 'incremental' the investment, the more likely this is to happen.

Perhaps a distinction should be drawn between an investment intended to increase the output of one homogeneous product (in which case it is self-evident that the return will be measured in relation to the whole output of that product by the firm in question) and some identifiably separate element of a system. It is in the latter case that confusion might arise.

In a way this may sound contradictory. Earlier I had been complaining that marginal 'fragmented' analysis was wrongly applied to problems of a whole industry. Yet here, in the investment decision context, the reverse seems to be the case: an analysis possibly applicable to a whole industry is misapplied to its sub-divisions. The paradox is only on the surface. The com-

F   81

mon error is a reluctance to analyse systems of interrelationships. An industry is seen only as the sum of its parts and this is as wrong in relation to the whole industry as it is to any fragments of which it is composed. Let me apply the logic of university student-staff ratios. If two universities in broadly similar situations find themselves with a ratio of 16:1 and 12:1 respectively, this is certainly a strong argument for adding to the staff of the first of these. If two departments of the *same* university show ratios of 16:1 and 12:1, the case becomes much more complicated; the university average is, and should be, compounded of ratios above and below the average, due to indivisibilities, complementarities and so on. In fact staff replacements are not determined primarily by such ratios, but much more on the basis of 'We only have one econometrician', or 'We must have another lecturer in romance philology', or 'McTavish's departure has left us weak in fluid mechanics'. In other words at disaggregated, genuinely marginal levels one usually seeks something specific. One cannot use a 'spare' lecturer in German in order to cover a gap in biochemistry, or vice versa.

The economy is like this too. Obviously so in the labour market (*pace* Mishan). Less obviously so, but so, in investment decisions. The point about systems and complexes made earlier must be stressed again. Some investment decisions are indeed of such a nature that they call for a decision about whether to have a given system or sub-system at all. Others are genuinely incremental, and can be properly presented as a choice of whether or not to add x per cent to existing capacity. Some are part of a larger whole, and are required, unless it is decided that the larger whole be scrapped or modified. A variant of this is the input-output concept; a given quantity of electric power or sulphuric acid is needed because of the expected requirements of the aluminium or chemical industry, for example. In still other cases the scale of the proposed investment is predetermined: a bridge must cross the river, the electrification of the line to Glasgow must reach Glasgow and not stop 40 miles short. Some investments require to get into a given time-sequence, and cannot be postponed without upsetting a larger programme.

Now of course no economist would deny any of this. Once again I can see someone exclaiming, 'Is this not unnecessarily breaking down an open door?' To which one can reply, 'Theory nowhere specifically denies that any of the above circumstances can and do occur'. However, it does tend to abstract from such matters, and students who learn about investment criteria generally do so in the usual one-dimensional way, and conclude that the scale of the project is a function of the financial returns attributable to that project. Not only students suffer from this form of myopia. One can read with some care through the report of the Select Committee on Nationalised Industries, including the expert evidence, and find no sense that investment decisions often occur within systems, within given objectives or purposes (which can be redefined in the light of information about costs, of course). The expected financial results, and the interest rate, can and should play a vital role in the process of choice between alternative means. Given that capacity of x Kw is needed, it can be provided in different ways. Bridges can be of different width and types of construction. Sulphuric acid can be produced in different places, in plants of varying size with varying equipment. One chooses the scheme which provides the required goods or service at least cost, or highest profit. This will often yield revenue well above the 'cut-off point', a possibility which theory as commonly taught associates with a 'rationing of investment capital', but which must be an extremely common occurrence, since no one in his right mind will invest more than is required to provide the needed facilities merely to bring the DCF to the 'right' level. In other words, indivisibilities will ensure considerable variations above the cut-off line, and complementarities ('internalities') will justify some investments below this line. If this is the case, and it often is, why should we as economists not say so loud and clear, in case some of our students eventually are called upon to advise decision-makers in the real world? In addition there is the problem of external effects, which should be of especial importance in the nationalised industries. But let us at least not ignore *internal* effects, as theorists far too easily do.

A critic might demur, 'What about cost-benefit analysis?'

Even the most pedestrian theorists refer to it nowadays, yet it has hardly been mentioned in all these pages. The criticism seems a just one, but only on the surface. Yes, the advocates of cost-benefit analysis are indeed concerned with the sort of benefits and costs which do not automatically show up in the market place, for were it otherwise there would be no need for this species of analysis. A case often quoted is the Victoria Line of the London Underground. In terms of net revenue it cannot pay, since most of its users travelled (less conveniently) by other routes operated by London Transport. But if congestion, queues and discomfort were given a monetary value, then it seems that the Victoria line was worth building.

Good. But several observations are in order. Firstly, few noted that the calculation was to some extent a substitute for competition. That is to say, if each rail line and bus service were in private hands, the new and more convenient one would have attracted passengers away from competitors. It might then have paid to invest in it. The comparison is with a situation where the revenue from the less convenient service accrued anyway to the same (public) corporation, and in these circumstances a service-improving investment can seldom be shown to pay. Let me use another illustration to prove the point. The huge air terminal in London is an awkward 600 yards or so from the nearest underground station. The underground line lies right beneath it. Suppose that to build a new station at this point costs £200,000. It would save many thousand people a tiresome walk with heavy cases, or a long wait in the taxi queue. A cost-benefit analysis might well show that this is £200,000 very well spent. But neither the airlines nor the transport undertaking have any financial interest in the matter, since their revenues are not significantly affected. Now imagine that BEA alone used that particular town terminal, while its competitors used another one which happened to be right on top of a station, say at Earls Court. Then there would be a competitive advantage ('Easier to go by Air France, you don't have to haul luggage so damn far'). *Then* it might well pay BEA to subsidise London Transport to have a new station right there under the West London air terminal. Just for this kind of reason TWA finds it worth while to do a deal with American customs to have extra officers posted at their terminal in New York's Kennedy airport, and to advertise the fact that you have less delay if you travel TWA. (BOAC has now done the same thing).

Now the second point. Cost-benefit analysis has not, to my knowledge, ever been discussed or applied in the context of internal economies, i.e. to the internal cost and benefits within a corporation. Indeed it has very largely been devoted to the 'translation' into monetary terms of social considerations, such as time-saving and congestion, or saving of life. Of course it is hardly possible to identify social benefits which are not also economic, and vice-versa. Perhaps the point is better made by contrasting these costs and benefits which of their nature *cannot* be handled in terms of any firm's profit-and-loss account, and those which depend on the answer to the question, 'Profitable for whom?' In the second case, profitability may depend on which system or sub-system one is considering. Hard-headed Swiss business men tolerate subsidies to tourist services (e.g. lake steamers) not because of love of amenity but because it *pays* to have efficient and ample services for tourists. If the Edinburgh festival brings £x million of business to Edinburgh, then a municipal subsidy is justified, apart from the virtues of the arts as such. Cost-benefit analysis also tends to discredit itself by some rather far-fetched monetarisation of benefits. Thus it is offensive to good sense and even morality to measure human life or loss of time by the victim's salary or future earning capacity. This suggests that a young PhD student who is run over must be valued at a sum many times higher than a professor about to retire, but the contrary is true in a traffic jam. If I earn five times as much as a junior lecturer and we are both delayed in traffic, it seems that my time is 'worth' five times as much as his even though we are both on the way to visit our respective girl-friends![37]

These analyses also suffer from the defect of attaching an arbitrary 'valuation' to subjective judgments. Thus airports create noise and other disutilities, but how much are these worth? The outcome of the calculation can be predetermined by the figure selected by the analyst. True, the analyst can reply that it is better to calculate than not to calculate, that a rough and questionable valuation may be better than no valuation at all. This is a matter of opinion. My personal view is that arbitrary valuations can too often disguise what are really value-judgments in the clothes of unreal quantification.

Such pseudo-computations have gone some way to discredit cost-benefit analysis. But clearly it is of great potential value, properly used. The trouble is that it has no effect unless in conjunction with a decision-making process. The Victoria Line could be built because the decision belonged to the Ministry of Transport and the Treasury. Unfortunately, this is a rare instance. The large number of decisions taken by public (and private) bodies which affect other firms and individuals cannot be the subject of cost-benefit analysis unless some institution exists to undertake it, and it has power to act. Otherwise we are in the realm of empty computations and ineffectual protests. We shall be discussing later on how these things could be more effectually organised. The problem should be soluble in the case of nationalised industries, because logically their very existence as *nationalised* industries should facilitate the solution. It is unfortunate that this point is overlooked in the efforts to make them truly 'commercial'.

It is as well to remind ourselves that the cost-benefit analysis which led to the building of the Victoria Line followed a proposal by the London Transport authority. They made the proposal not because they expected that it would pay, but precisely because they felt that theirs was the responsibility for improving transport facilities in London, i.e. a species of 'social contract' with Londoners, which Mr Munby decried. Unless, in other words, the authority charged with providing a good or service is trying to carry out its function, it is unlikely to initiate proposals which can then be considered by cost-benefit analysis.

This same point was made by P. D. Henderson. Arguing that it is both unrealistic and wrong to expect public enterprises to 'define their own interests in purely financial terms', he pointed out that 'the specialised knowledge and experience which the enterprises possess will usually be needed if informed estimates

of the size of external effects are to be made', and refers specifically to the Victoria Line.[38]

We have wandered far from theory proper. So perhaps we
could end this section with a recapitulation of arguments on
monopoly theory. It should and could be made clear that it is
not just a question of profit maximisation, achieved by marginal
adjustments of the quantity and price of a homogeneous
product. We all should know the meaning of the phrase
'sellers' market' and its consequences. A monopolist, in so far
as he is a monopolist, is in a strong position as a seller. Consequently he can neglect quality, provide poor service, not
bother about punctual deliveries, tolerate queues, subordinate
the convenience of the customer to his own, keep the minimum
of stocks, limit choice, and all this could be profitable for him,
or else fit with the 'satisficing' hypothesis, since the single-
minded pursuit of profit is an exhausting business and the
monopolist could well dislike the rat-race. Once this is accepted,
it follows that criteria for 'commercial' operation of nationalised
monopolies should be given much more careful scrutiny than
they now receive. As for oligopoly, competition limited to a few
giants, one is uneasily aware that Shubik is right, that 'There is
no oligopoly theory.'[39] And yet again, 'When we deal with
problems of quality and service, not only do we not have
good measures, but very often we do not have even a good
dimensional analysis to describe the units of measurement. For
example, what are the dimensions in which we should measure a
good transportation service?'[40] What indeed . . . ? Similar ideas
can also be found in the work of Helmut Arndt, of the University of Berlin. In his 'Oekonomische Theorie der Macht'[41] he
emphasises the deficiencies of conventional monopoly and
monopoly theory, confined as it is to the two variables of price
and quality of a homogeneous product. In fact, he insists,
powerful firms can alter the 'data' or parameters in a number of
ways, up to and including influencing the rules made by public
authorities. They can seek to minimise their own risks, thereby
increasing the costs of those dependent on them. They can vary
conditions of payment. They can increase profits also by
worsening the quality of the product or after-sales service. They

can reduce choice and the number of distribution points, restrict durability, alter productive capacity to suit themselves, concentrate on the goods and services most convenient (least costly) to produce, to the detriment of the consumer. They can obstruct the emergence of new and better products, or higher productivity 'to avoid costs arising from obsolescence of existing production layout, or on grounds of bureaucratic inertia (comfort) (*bequemlichkeit*) or to avoid unnecessary risk. . . .'[42] Note that Arndt is discussing big private business. A *fortiori* management of nationalised industries can act in such ways too.

Yet how little understanding our typical economic advisers have of such matters as these! How else can one explain the Post Office's powers as a 'commercial' corporation. I can do no better than reprint the following extract from a well-informed newspaper report.

'. . . it has been a great deal easier for the Post Office to bump up charges since the Post Office Act of 1969 which turned the GPO into a supposedly commercial corporation. In the bad old days Parliament had to vet all price increases. Now all that is necessary is for the Post Office to consult POUNC, the Post Office Users' National Council, and then—one day before applying the new rates—to announce its intention in the official gazettes of Belfast, Edinburgh and London.

'What this freedom in price-fixing can mean in practice has already been demonstrated in a tragi-comedy of errors which ended earlier this year. In 1970 the Post Office increased telephone charges retrospectively, on many bills describing the extra money now due as "arrears".

'Dozens of subscribers, enraged by what they considered a clear breach of commercial practice and spurred on by the Independent Telephone Users' Association, refused to pay up. To their astonishment it was clearly demonstrated by legal advisers that under the 1969 Act, the Post Office had power to do not only this but a good deal more.

'Meanwhile, it has yet to dawn on the public that the Post Office is totally exempted from the main disciplines of normal commercial practice. Specifically, there is no contractual

88

relationship between the Post Office and its private users. This means that whatever the Post Office does (more or less), it cannot be sued.

'At a time when Parliament has been at pains to outlaw the unfair shedding of traders' liabilities, it is curious that the Post Office—a complete monopoly now being hailed as a commercial enterprise and incidentally the biggest business in the land—has itself been permitted to shed all direct responsibility to its users.'[43]

I submit that the 'philosophy' underlying the Post Office Act of 1969 would have been different had the authorities employed Arndt and Nove as advisers, instead of the conventional and one-dimensional X and Y (Who were they?). Badly understood theory has bad practical effects.

In fact a Conservative government has hearkened unto the POUNC, and has prevented the Post Office from simultaneously reducing services and increasing charges. This was hardly in the spirit of the Act; fortunately for the public it was not!

Perhaps it is worth a few lines to dispose of a red herring. Some of the modern literature on monopoly insists that, by means of product differentiation, many producers turn themselves into monopolists for their own products. In a sense this is so. Only one firm produces Blubbo shampoo. However, the point (as Arndt points out) is the *power* of a given firm to alter quantity, price, quality, service, availability, etc. In this sense Blubbo is but one shampoo among others, and its management operates in a competitive environment which leaves it little room for manoeuvre. Of course no one is a total and unconditional monopolist, except possibly the Post Office (but even then, there are carrier pigeons). Yet this is a real problem of monopoly all the same.

Several economists with whom I have discussed these problems react sympathetically to the arguments, but reply along the following lines. Even if all that is so, there will still be a preference for conventional micro-economics, because it is a coherent and rigorous theory; the views expressed here do not add up to an alternative theory.

I am not sure that there is much force in this objection.

Suppose, to take an example, someone had developed a model of the functioning of a planned economy and chose to assume that planners were perfectly informed about the plans and productive potential of a limited number of enterprises, each of which made one homogeneous product. Suppose that I were to challenge this model, on the grounds that the economy is large and complex, so that planners are often misinformed because managers are interested in persuading their bosses to give them a plan that is easy to fulfil, and also that the adjustment of managers of multi-product firms to aggregated plans causes major distortions in the product mix. It would surely not be legitimate simply to dispose of these objections on the grounds that I had no 'rigorous' model to replace the one I was challenging. A model which draws attention away from certain complexities is of little use in circumstances in which these very complexities are the object of study. In our case what seems to be called for is a 'marriage' between systems analysis and the marginal-incremental approach, plus a much-needed emphasis on interdependencies, complementarities, purpose, function, objectives—objective functions if one prefers this term. All this is still on a formal, abstract level. It will not help anyone to take an actual decision about electricity, shipyards, buses or widgets, since this requires the application of generalised ideas to particular circumstances. But a student brought up so might have his attention directed towards important matters which at present tend to be left out of sight.

But, the critic will repeat, where is the alternative *theory*? Alas, I am hardly capable of writing a textbook of economics with a systematic exposition of the systems-economics which is needed. Whatever theory is devised would lack the formal elegance of the Walras-Pareto model and its many modern derivatives. But it is surely the case that this elegance is a precondition for its inapplicability, and vice versa. Generalisation requires abstraction, but it also requires to be judged by the test of relevance, of its value-in-use.

'Negative criticism', some of my colleagues will say. 'No doubt life is full of complexities, and mistakes can be made. But what does this author suggest? Is he denying the importance of economic efficiency as a criterion for operating nationalised industries? Is he trying to turn them into social services? Surely this is going back to the woolly 'forties, abandoning in the process many hard-learned lessons about operational criteria'.

Very well. Let me start to answer the critics.

No, one should not be woolly, and electricity, transport, gas, television, posts, should be operated on economic criteria, in the sense that there should be most careful regard to cost and revenues. It is right and proper always to ask if the proposed expenditure is justified, is there not some other and more profitable use for resources, which will yield more benefits for society? There must also be some intersection between the financial results of any given public enterprise and the kind and extent of the goods and services which it provides or ought to provide.

1 *A definition of function and purpose*   What is the nationalised industry set up for? What ought it to be doing? This, as already argued, is the concept of 'role' towards which the market guides a firm under competition, but which needs to be spelt out as a *duty* in a public corporation. In other words, economic operation must be subject to the *constraint* of performing the purposes for which the corporation exists as a public body. How these constraints are to be defined, who is to do the defining, are important practical questions to which we will return.

2 *The public interest must be part of the operational principles*, and not an external element spasmodically imposed. That is to say, even if a supervising or regulating body exists, the definition of the corporation's task, the way in which it sees itself and briefs its own junior officials, must emphasise quality and service. Here again, under competition it can be argued that good quality and service pay. This is not so under a monopoly. When the SNCF announces publicly that it aims to ensure that passengers leaving Paris at the Easter holiday rush have seats on the trains, or the Dutch railways take pride in claiming that all goods handed in or collected on any day will be delivered to any

destination in Holland the next day, they are imposing standards on themselves. This is an alternative to having some outside body impose them. It will not happen by some miraculous automatism mislabelled 'commercial operation', conceived vulgarmarginalistically at that.

3 *Any system will have some loss-making as well as profit-making activities*, and consequently it is the overall financial result that counts. It may be, in some circumstances, that a subsidy would prove desirable. Thus San Francisco voters may opt for a rapid-transit system which is planned to operate at a loss, if only because, at 'economic' fares, it would fail in its purpose to provide an alternative for overloaded super-highways. But even if the rapid-transit system could be made to pay, we may be sure that *parts* of it would 'lose money'. In other words, any conceivable design of a transport network, any set of subway lines projected in any conurbation, would yield a mixture of profit and loss, and therefore no network could be designed other than in its entirety. The public or its representa-tives in fact consider what kind of rapid-transit system is wanted; this is costed, and the plans modified, and in the end some variant is chosen as a whole. This is surely what happens, or ought to happen, if one starts from nothing, as is the case in San Francisco, Köln, Munich, Vienna, Leningrad and other places where underground systems are being built. They are not viewed as a sum of incremental decisions. This is a typical instance of the inadequacy and indeed confusion of marginal analysis of the conventional type. It is true, naturally, that in the process of deciding what network to build in San Francisco, one does say, 'Shall this line be extended beyond Berkeley, or how far northwards should that other line go?' But these are incre-mental decisions *within the system*, which does not consist of the sum of them, since the decision to have a system at all imposes its own context and limits the alternatives. (Of course, in a sense, to have the San Francisco rapid-transit system at all is a 'marginal' decision. However, this is stretching words too far, surely, at least too far for conventional micro-economics, whose instinct is always to unpick the package. In any case, it

really is a misuse of language to apply the term 'marginal' to a decision of this magnitude.) The point being made is logically similar to the one made earlier about universities. Even if we agree that the San Francisco rapid-transit system should be subject to the same criteria as the rest of the economy, i.e. it requires some minimum rate of return on capital (including de-congestion and reduced pollution among the benefits), this rate should apply to the system, and *cannot* apply to all parts of it. If this entails 'cross-subsidisation', that is just too bad.

4 *Clear thinking on subsidies is essential* This means, certainly, avoiding confusion over cross-subsidisation, and therefore a rational view of pricing within the system, of which more will be said in moment. I have in mind here the question of subsidy to the system as a whole. The objections are well known and weighty. It might entail an open-ended commitment. It is no spur to efficiency. It is hard to find a rational basis for such charges as are levied. Thus if costs are covered at £1 and the charge is 0·80, why should it not be 0·60, 0·40, or any sum arbitrarily chosen by reference to a vaguely defined social objective? In any case, the concealment of real costs can and must distort resource allocation. This constitutes a sound argument for avoiding net subsidies, except where a strong case exists in favour. Such a case can only rest on an intelligently-applied cost benefit analysis, in the course of which it is shown that important beneficiaries do not pay for the goods or services provided. This needs careful examination in each case. Thus (abstracting from problems of pollution) one cannot really assert that all the users of electricity, coal, steel, ought to be subsidised through artificially low prices for any of these commodities. To do so would affect the choice of fuels, and discourage measures to economise in their use. We will discuss in a moment the question of what is an economic price for a nationalised industry to charge and who should decide it, but whatever it is, it should apply to fuels. (This still leaves open the questions of peak demand or consumers located in remote places. I am speaking here of the total price in relation to total costs.) Things are much more complex in the case of transport

93

services, and what could be called cultural amenities. Let us look at them in detail to identify principles.

Does public transport benefit only those who use it? Clearly not. If an additional 20 per cent of London residents decided to use cars instead of trams or buses, traffic would jam, and few could get to work. So among the beneficiaries are those who go to work by car and never use the public system at all. The existence of a rapid-transit system benefits owners of property, of shops, offices, factories, indeed anyone whose workers and customers have to get about. Imagine defending the proposition that only those who use the *vaporetti* in Venice benefit from their existence. Suppose all hotel-owners and shopkeepers have private motor-boats, are they not also major beneficiaries? If a cruise liner docks at a port, should port charges not be influenced by the fact that passengers will spend money ashore? (I understand that the management of one Scottish port failed to see this; perhaps it had been reading books on micro-economics. A cruise liner decided never to call again, because charges were so high. Who lost? Only the docks?)

The other example is urban amenity in general. Here we tend to be victims of conservatism. Museums and public parks never 'pay', and no one supposes that they should, whether or not admission charges are levied. In Germany the same tradition applies also to opera and drama. Munich is aware that its image as a cultural centre (with a new underground rail system to boot) attracts business by projecting an attractive goodwill-type image. This affects the profitability of many urban businesses and also city revenues in general. It is not only a value-judgment about the desirability of culture (though personally I see nothing wrong with the proposition that *Die Zauberflöte* is better than the Rolling Stones).

Public subsidies for opera and music do now exist in Britain, but, despite Lord Robbins's association with Covent Garden, economists as a profession have done little to help and much to hinder this development. With the Conservative government's present ethos, we may well owe the preservation of cultural subsidies to the accident that Mr Heath is musical. At municipal level it is very much an uphill struggle. 'Incremental' economics seem to reinforce the blinkers which grow naturally on some councillors.

In the field of transport it is almost funny to observe the convolutions of otherwise intelligent men. Aware of the problem of congestion, they try to handle it without committing the sin of subsidy, by proposing appropriate charges for road use. In itself the idea of making charges is, needless to say, a sound one. The economists concerned are aware that taxing the actual vehicles is not an effective solution, because people are influenced in the use of the vehicles they already possess by the marginal cost of that particular journey. So they try to add to the cost of private car or lorry travel. This is already done to some extent by car parking charges, but this is indeed not enough. So they imagine every road in urban areas wired, and a little black box in every car registering road use at different times of the day. Mr A. in his car who travels in central London between (say) 9 am and 8 pm will pay so much for the time he spends there in his car. Presumably the man who travels into the centre of Glasgow or Plymouth would pay too, but less, since the congestion is less, while the one who goes into the village of Little Puddlesbury from his farm will pay nothing, as in that area there is no congestion problem at all.

Technologically the little black box is feasible. But administratively, socially, politically, it is a nightmare. Residents? Invalids? Tourists, foreign? Tourists from other areas of Britain? Doctors? Nurses? Imagine the administration of rebates and exemptions, the outcry, the unpopularity. Proper car parking charges, enforcement of parking regulations, the banning of certain streets to traffic, all these are very sensible and desirable measures, which can win acceptance politically. But this will still leave it a fact that the services rendered by public transport far exceed those rendered to the individuals who purchase tickets. So a pricing doctrine which is rational on the assumption that this is *not* the case is still not applicable, whatever taxes and levies affect private cars. The economists who advance black box type solutions are, by temperament, those who would substitute a differential charge for a 'No entry' or 'No right turn' sign, if only such things were even remotely feasible.

Who should pay a subsidy, if there is to be one? That is a complex question. No reason why a subsidy for London should be paid by taxpayers residing in the north of Scotland. The difficulty is that many users do not reside in the areas which administer the services. Thus millions of visitors use London Transport and thousands of non-residents go to Covent Garden for opera and ballet. Glasgow's municipal services are used by non-residents too. Ships or buses which serve the islands and highlands of Scotland are used also by tourists from London and, for that matter from Hamburg. In the case of services provided by a national or regional system, there is further difficulty caused by the allocation of overheads in computing local costs, and the locally-generated contribution to the revenue of the rest of the system. These are not, of course, arguments against a principle, merely great difficulties which stand in the way of its rational and acceptable application.

The Transport Act of 1968 did indeed provide for Passenger Transport Authorities with regional responsibility and some now exist in various combinations in England. They can operate services at a loss and collect the money from local authorities in their area. What causes concern is the advice some economists would give these authorities: to abandon unprofitable services unless specifically subsidised.

I have already argued at length that the application of such principles to urban transportation rapidly reduces itself to a nonsense, if applied to particular routes or times. It is nonsensical as well as impracticable for the authority whose job is to provide transport for Norwich, or New York, or Marseilles, or Leningrad, to seek a separate subsidy for the No. 21 bus because it is not profitable! However, it is plausible to argue that non-urban transport is different. Suppose that Oban is connected with Glasgow, or Oberammergau with Munich, by rail lines which make a loss. Why should not the county or town pay for this loss? Why should not the county of Sussex pay for those rural services which the (publicly-owned) Southdown bus company cannot operate at a profit? In the earlier pages I gave the example of the hotel on an island served by a boat. If the boat were separately owned and there was a threat to remove it, then surely the hotel would subsidise the boatman. Is this not a proper analogy?

Yes and no. A profitable system, as already argued, includes some 'loss-making' parts in most cases. Urban transportation is only a tighter, more interlinked system, but the Deutsche Bundesbahn (or Lufthansa, or whatever) is also a system. The identification of the separate loss on the service to Oberammergau or Oban is so complex that no one even publishes the calculation, and so no one is ever satisfied with the figure. The beneficiaries will always include persons who are not within the area which is being asked to pay the subsidy. So for national networks there is usually a strong case for a subsidy out of the central exchequer, if any is to be paid at all, while urban services might have to be the subject of a graduated regional levy of some kind.

Shepherd would probably agree with these arguments, for he sees many problems involved in 'direct subsidies for certain "social" activities of the public corporations.' Among them, as already argued above, is that of identifying 'which activities are "social" and which are "commercial"', and he points out that this method is actually '*more* likely to encourage public-firm inefficiency than would cross-subsidising', because—if I understand his argument aright—it would tie the corporation down to specifically subsidised activities, whereas with a lump-sum subsidy it would try to recast its productive or service activities to maximise their effectiveness.[44] Shepherd's views seem close to those of another critic of orthodoxy in these matters, Henderson, who puts the point as follows; 'It has sometimes been suggested that the only clear and satisfactory procedure is for public enterprises to act according to strict "commercial" principles, as though they were private corporations, and thus to maximise profits subject to certain rules, constraints or instructions—which are laid down by the government.' He does not agree, any more than I do. 'It is more sensible,' he says, to try to 'induce enterprises to take a wider view, rather than maintaining a pretence that their only proper concern is with the financial consequences to themselves of their actions.' This is, as already mentioned, because no one can know better than the management how best to run the service as a whole; they can often see the external effects better than the government, and so are in the best position to make the best use of a general subsidy, if one is given. The point is made, rightly, that public corporations can go too far in cross-subsidising in the name of an undefined public interest, and that duties require to be defined by the authorities. However, 'critics of past mistakes have sometimes gone too far in asserting that the sole concern of these enterprises should be with profitability...'.[45]

An exceptional justification for a purely local subsidy for a portion of a line can exist, indeed. One example is taken from the San Francisco area. The original scheme proposed that, to save cost, the trains should run on elevated tracks through Berkeley. Berkeley residents protested. Very well, replied the rapid transit authority, it would cost $x million to put them underground, will you pay the difference? Berkeley had a poll and the vote was 'Yes', so they paid the difference. Note, however, that the benefit was purely Berkeley's. Seldom are there such 'pure' cases as this.

What of the objections that a subsidy means an open-ended commitment? Surely the answer is not to make it open-ended. This is by no means easy, but there are precedents. In some cities the transport authority does not have to meet interest payments, or track costs, but must cover operational costs. Some theatre buildings are provided free by the city, but the drama company must meet its salary, costumes, and scenery bill. There are many choices. None of them are free from criticism.

One way is the French way. As any visitor to France knows, many French civilians carry cards entitling them to large reductions in fares on the railway. These relate to annual holidays, large families, education, old age and so on. A British analogy is reduced-fare tickets for members of the armed forces. These are all ways of subsidising passengers, but the payment is not made to the passengers but to the railway (e.g. by the social security department, or the Ministry of War). This helps to fill the trains (indeed at holiday time to overfill them), and does so by deliberately giving advantages to certain groups of citizens. So one can achieve the welfare advantage of utilising a downward-sloping marginal cost curve, while at the same time it is then possible to ask the railway to cover its costs out of its revenues, including in the latter the payments received from government departments.

Some have argued that urban transport facilities could be free, i.e. wholly paid for by local taxation, since the services rendered are to the whole city, including non-users. There would be a marked saving in administrative and accounting costs and it may be doubted whether demand would significantly increase. After the novelty wore off, few would take bus or underground rides merely for the fun of it. Perhaps more logical and practical would be a charge which met variable costs. It is perhaps justifiable to advocate such a method of charging as a means of ensuring full utilisation of the facilities available. An under-used train or bus is evidence of a downward-sloping marginal cost curve, since evidently the extra costs incurred in carrying additional passengers would be very small, and this situation would accord with a textbook example of a rational subsidy, as well as contributing to external economies via decongestion. This would mean covering capital cost out of national or local taxes. It is important to stress in this connection that people benefit from transportation in cities in their capacities as parents (children go to school or visiting without requiring to be taken), hosts (visitors can get to them more easily), husbands (wife can go shopping and visiting without a second car), shopkeepers, and even as themselves (car breaks down), whether or not they are regular travellers on public service vehicles. It *may* therefore be not all that wrong to visualise paying for transportation as one pays for water, through local taxes of some kind. One objection, however, relates to the effect this would have on peak-hour travel, which ought somehow to be discouraged, and rises in local taxes are seldom very popular. It is not suggested that we know for sure what *the* answer to such problems is. Only we must think of them as a whole, and not seek to escape from them by fragmented incrementalism.

Chapter 5

Pricing and Investment Criteria

A simple proposition: if prices in nationalised industries are to be limited or controlled, as they surely should be, then they cannot be used as a basis for comparing profitability with a price-control-free and profit-making private industry. The need for price control in the nationalised sector arises, surely, from the quasi-monopoly situation of most of them. If this is accepted, and if this is the normal practice in most countries, it is remarkable indeed to find that many economists insist on identical criteria in the nationalised and private sectors. In so insisting they seem to carry the 'Pareto' outlook about with them: in such a world as that it would indeed be true that we would be comparing alternatives on a comparable basis. But if (say) demand for electricity is rising and the industry could increase its prices by 20 per cent and thereby increase its profits, but is limited to an increase of 5 per cent, then obviously *any* comparison between the profitability of a decision concerning electricity generation and other branches of the economy could lead to misleading results.

This question of prices raises two different kinds of problems. The first is the rationale of price control in nationalised industries. Ought they to be set free? Some might argue so. My belief is that control is inescapable if and when competition is weak. It is surely not the case that nationalised enterprises are, or ought to be, profit-maximisers. Theoretically they could be instructed, *à la* Lange, to behave as if they were operating under competitive conditions, but for reasons already discussed this cannot really be practicable. Some species of price control must usually exist. But whether the price restraint is voluntary or compulsory, it must affect computations of profitability, whether these relate to today or to five years hence, since the management must assume that it, unlike private enterprise, will have only limited freedom to charge high.

This leads at once to the second problem. In seeking to impose identical criteria on nationalised and private sectors, economists are seeking to find some basis for a rational allocation of resources between them. If there are choices to be made, between investments in (public) transport, gas, electricity, water and, on the other hand, in (private) cars, chemicals, clothing and real estate, how can one choose without criteria applicable to all these (and other) sectors?

This seems a strong argument, yet if one approaches it closely one sees holes in it. One of these, relating to interest rates and their significance, will be examined closely in a moment. We must accept, of course, the trivial but true point that we ought to do those things that most need doing. This is also the case if the choice is between building another school, hospital, road or university laboratory. We try to rank them, to make the best choice, and we frequently fail. Nationalised industries are also 'competitors' for scarce resources. If one decides to provide piped water to a new housing scheme, or to build the San Francisco rapid transit system, one is indeed taking a political decision, which could be faulted by 'optimising' perfectionists because—who knows?—the resources *could* have been better used. What has happened is that a political process has been decisive, and rightly so. We do *not* say, because clothing and real estate 'earn' more than water and rapid-transit, one should shift resources into clothing and real estate. In the private sector this could (and perhaps should) happen. But surely, in the case of the nationalised sector, the state's very role is justified precisely because non-identical criteria apply? To say this is to define the problem more clearly, not to solve it, because—agreed!—choices have to be made, opportunity-cost is a fact. Judgment must be made in the knowledge of costs and benefits. But the first step is to see through the 'identical criteria' fallacy.

Then how much capital ought the nationalised sector as a whole to have? It is not enough to say that the decision should be 'political', since economists may well be asked by politicians for advice. Yet it must be admitted that no precise answer is possible. No one in his right mind would refuse to supply water to a housing project because a higher rate of return would be earned elsewhere; (it is a typical 'not-what-but-how' kind of investment decision, or else it can be seen as subsumed within the housing project viewed as a sub-system). It is not so very different to say that electricity investment must be such as to ensure adequate supplies to meet needs at anticipated levels of demand at the probable price. The trouble is that the state sector as a whole includes both saleable goods and services and sectors which do not sell in a market. Some of the saleable goods, as we have already noted, are essential inputs for private industry and for households. Some goods can be imported if there proves to be a shortage of them, others (like electricity) can create a serious bottleneck situation if demand exceeds estimates. One must consider the input-output logic of the expected pattern of growth, on the basis of which one can attempt forecasts. The share of the state sector in total invest-ment will then depend (in large part, at least) on the extent to which the anticipated inputs are provided by the public sector. It would make no sense to have some *a priori* view on the share of nationalised industries in investments of this type. As for investments in housing, schools, hospitals, roads, this is every-where a matter of political decision, in the sense that neither the profit-and-loss account nor input-output logic govern decisions such as these. More thought is necessary about this subject, which we will not pursue further here. To know that there is yet no satisfactory answer is, probably, a shade better than to think one has an answer which happens, alas, to be wrong.

What is the role of prices in taking investment decisions? To-day's prices are scarcely of much use as indicators for building power stations which will be completed in 5–7 years' time. It is difficult to fit the decision-making to any *marginal* calculus, save in the trivial sense that one is discussing the incremental (additional) generating capacity which will be needed in five or seven years' time and thereafter. Additional power stations, or the current they generate, are unlikely to be more expensive, so the long-run marginal cost curve has no reason to slope upwards, and may even fall, with the introduction of modern cost-saving techniques. The decisive factors, surely, are first and foremost a correct estimate of user demand (industrial and domestic), and, linked with it, the cost and output trends of competing fuels. Prices are relevant; prices and costs of electricity as projected into the future, and also prices of competing fuels; indeed, also prices and costs of the products of major power users. If, for instance, natural gas supplies will rise swiftly, and costs decline, these are reasons for adverse effects on demand for electricity for heating, but perhaps a positive effect on costs of production if electricity generation uses natural gas or a fuel. If all these computations work out right, then the investments will probably yield the desired discounted cash flow, rate of return, present value or whatever.

Here, as so often, Joan Robinson is on the right lines. 'Future demands, as supplies are increased, form an integrated pattern... There is no way in which [the investor] can declare a pattern of future prices and then allow the pattern of investment to work itself out on the basis of maximising profits. The pattern of investment and the pattern of future prices have to be worked out as a single operation.' She holds that 'atomistic competition and correct foresight are irremediably irreconcilable', thereby emphasising the importance of locating investment decisions within a complex of investment plans. Investment is no field for Walras's *tâtonnement*, i.e. trial and error. One must calculate on paper 'until a fit is achieved. Once the fit has been found, the plan must be put into operation as a whole. Each individual enterprise has to accept its part in the scheme. Errors have to be corrected on paper, not embodied in bricks and steel before they are found out.'[46] The key factor surely is *uncertainty*, about the future decisions of consumers and about plant, technical changes and tax burdens affecting oil, nuclear energy, gas and the like. As Simon puts it in an excellent survey article, 'The classical theory [or rather the neoclassical orthodoxy A. N.] is a theory of a man choosing among fixed and known alternatives, to each of which is attached known consequences.'[47] Of course, all economists know that the real world is not like t, and yet their theories tend repeatedly to abstract from the ract that the future is not known.

Uncertainty about the future is a much more important source of error than differences in methods of computation (e.g. internal rate of return versus DCF). But such mistakes will not be averted by analysis in terms of existing prices, and one's (fallible) estimates of the future would in any case enter into price (and cost) estimates relative to a situation in five years' time, in the process of assessing likely levels of demand.

How well this was put by that wise economist Tjalling Koopmans (and how little effect on theory his words seem to have had!): 'To my knowledge no formal model of resource allocation through competitive markets has been developed, which recognises ignorance about all decision makers' future actions, preferences or states of technological information as the main source of uncertainty confronting each individual decision maker, and which at the same time acknowledges the fact that forward markets on which anticipations and intentions could be tested and adjusted do not exist in sufficient variety and with a sufficient span of foresight to make presently developed theory regarding the efficiency of competitive markets applicable. If this judgment is correct, our economic knowledge has not yet been carried to the point where it sheds much light on the main problem of the economic organisation of society; the problem of how to face and deal with uncertainty. In particular *the economics profession is not ready to speak with anything approaching scientific authority on the economic aspects of the issue of individual versus collective enterprise which divides mankind in our time.*'[48]

G. B. Richardson made a similar point in a different but equally telling way: 'Under perfect competition it would be quite impossible for any firm to know how much of a good to produce. According to the usual story, entrepreneurs are guided by prices; each of them sets an output which equates the price of the good he sells to its marginal cost. Now it is clear that current prices cannot be the appropriate signals . . . about what to produce in the future. Presumably, therefore, firms are supposed to equate marginal costs to future prices.

But how then is a producer to predict future prices, depending as they do on the demands of the consumers and on the supply plans of all his competitors? This the textbooks do not tell us. . . . If the future price of a good were known to be greater than the current cost of making it, then a profit opportunity may be said to exist; but if there are an unlimited number of firms able to respond to the opportunity, no individual firm will know what to do. A profit opportunity equally available to everyone is in fact available to none at all.'[49] It follows that perfect competition is not only non-existent but unworkable, and that attempts to simulate it are not the right way to deal with problems of nationalised industries. This underlines, too, the importance of *information*.

C. J. Hitch is equally forthright, and in being forthright he very properly reminds us that we should not ask our theories or methodology to perform feats of impossible perfectionism: 'What does the operational researcher do? Here he is, faced with his fundamental difficulty. The future is uncertain, Nature is unpredictable and his enemies and allies even more so. . . . How can he find the optimal course of action to recommend to his decision-maker?

'The simple answer is that he probably cannot. The same answer is also the beginning of wisdom in this business. There has altogether been too much obsession with optimisation on the part of operations researchers. . . . Most of our relations are so unpredictable that we do well to get the right sign and order of magnitude of the first differential. In most of our attempted optimisations we are kidding our customers, or ourselves, or both. If we can show our customer how to make a better decision than he otherwise would have made, we are doing well and all that can reasonably be expected of us.'[50] That makes sense. Let us leave optima to the textbooks. Or rather, let us remove from textbooks any implication that optima are identifiable, let alone attainable, in real life.

A reader might say, 'Well, all these quotations from responsible economists prove that the profession *is* aware of the problems here discussed, and so why all the fuss?' The answer is that these ideas are in a sense recognised as more or less legitimate comment, yet are as water off a duck's back: the dominant orthodoxy survives almost unscathed. To *accept* the validity of the challenge is to be compelled to revise a whole intellectual system (and rewrite a great many lecture courses!).

So it follows that current orthodox doctrine on investment choice is defective, both because it equates the nationalised price-controlled sector with an uncontrolled private sector, and because it has much less to say about the key element— uncertainty—than about the relatively insignificant (but methodologically interesting) niceties of computation of rates of return. It is hardly necessary to argue the proposition that the considerations relating to electricity in the above example apply in some degree to other industries too, and must affect investment decisions wherever the decision-maker is responsible for all, or a large segment of, productive capacity for the given item, and therefore must try to calculate the *total* demand for the given product in several years' time. This would be less important if the decision were being taken by a small entre- preneur in a competitive market, since he would be more interested in his competitiveness *vis-a-vis* his rivals than in the *total* demand for his product. As already said, indecisions relating to inputs vital to many industries, demand and the consequent investment decisions derive more from an input- output table (appropriately corrected for technological change) than from DCF analysis or discount rates.

Let us continue. It is unnecessary to do more than refer to the point made so often before, that the investment in question may well be part of a system, and that therefore a computation of profitability must relate to the whole as well as to the part. Also that 'system' must be understood as meaning not only physical-technological relationships (inputs, productive pro- cesses, etc) but also matters concerned with quality, goodwill and function. An investment may reduce queues, provide shelter in bad weather, enable one to supply all customers with the goods or service quickly and punctually. As was said earlier, conventional monopoly theory fails to point out that such activities do not necessarily pay, in fact seldom pay, unless the customer can turn to a competitor or has some effective countervailing power.

In case any reader has doubts as to whether these comments are superfluous, let us quote from a paper by Stewart Joy, Chief Economist of British Rail, about how to apply DCF criteria. 'In a productive process as complex and interactive as a railway system even the DCF criterion is not always easy to apply [sic]. . . . Many projects which are relatively small in physical terms, have a massive influence on the profitability of the continued use of related assets. [Yes indeed! A. N.]. . . . At first there was a tendency to except such projects from the 10 per cent present value criterion, on the grounds that they were 'essential' renewals. . . . The invalidity of this approach is obvious. [Is it?] It was thus not possible to accept without question the desirability of carrying out minor replacement projects on the ground that, if they were not done, a larger part of railway activity would be impeded. [Not 'without question', of course, but what better grounds are there!?] 'Ideally, such investments should include an analysis of the net cash flow for the total operation concerned.' [Surely not *only* the operation concerned, but apparently even this may not be done.] The *system* aspect seems oddly underplayed. Perhaps it is by such logic as this that British Rail has eliminated most sidings, thereby losing a considerable amount of goods traffic to the roads. Each such siding can *only* be justified in terms of 'influence on the profitability of continued use of related assets!'[51]

Finally there is the question of the meaningfulness of interest rates as a guide to time-preference; this is seen in two ways. Firstly, at a time of inflation and uncertainty, what do interest rates in fact represent? A guess at future inflation? Why should they be a sound guide to investment alternatives? In the days of stable prices, government bonds were at a lower interest rate than commercial-industrial shares, so it was thought that raising money for state ventures in the gilt-edged market would mean cheaper borrowing, presumably because of the virtual absence of risk. Now the situation is reversed. A further complication is that private corporations reinvest their profits at notional rates which seem (in practice) lower than the rate at which money can be raised in the market. It sounds sensible and even 'rigorous' to assert that nationalised industries ought to earn the same rate of return as any other industry, but the choice of the norm (say 10 per cent) is nonetheless arbitrary, the more so as it might change radically long before the project under discussion is completed.

Yet there is a second way of looking at the question. Take electricity again. Suppose that the likely demand for electricity in 1977 is estimated as being 20 per cent greater than today, so that capacity should be increased accordingly. Or that London needs a new underground line to relieve congestion. In what sense should this decision be influenced by interest rates? Suppose these go up from 6 per cent to 12 per cent, or down from 12 per cent to 6 per cent. Ought one then to refrain from building enough power stations? True, if one envisages a high rate as being due to a high level of demand for capital, this would be an argument for postponing projects until demand for capital (and capital goods) is less intense, reflecting perhaps some slack in the economy. But we do not seem to be living in this sort of world today. High interest rates and 'slack' coexist, or can coexist, because of inflationary price rises.

Investment decisions in the public sector must also be affected by 'political' choices. Is this a non-economic or unsound formulation? Not in the sense used here. Suppose we accept that one important reason for nationalisation is that the public interest and micro-profitability frequently fail to coincide in the sectors in question. Then it is for the government to ensure, directly, or through supervisory bodies, or by introducing legal constraints or obligations, that the public interest is taken into account also in investment decisions. To some extent this happens, in Britain and elsewhere. But theory is shy about admitting it, and theorists are apt to give advice which abstracts from these considerations. They could enter into cost-benefit analysis, provided that such analysis is not excessively fragmented and one is open about admitting value judgments. Thus postal deliveries in remote areas, the avoidance of power cuts on cold days, the provision of bus shelters to keep the rain off passengers, many matters concerned with regional policy and urban amenities, require investments which will usually not seem to 'pay' by normal commercial criteria, but which may none the less be justified either on grounds of public policy or on an appropriate 'cost-benefit' valuation (how much is it 'worth' not to get wet waiting for a bus, or not having dinner spoilt by a power-cut, or not having people move from Scotland to the south of England in search of a job? One can scarcely avoid some, possibly disguised, value judgments).

Or let us return to the London underground railway, or Edinburgh opera theatre, or some other durable and desirable asset. Suppose the interest rate to be 11 per cent, and the expected life of the asset is 100 years. It is to be enjoyed or used by our children and our children's children. The state is, to a greater extent than the private investor, concerned with the future. A high discount rate may well reflect a high degree of uncertainty, which quite legitimately makes the private investor prefer short-term ventures. Why should this cause the *state* to prefer short-term ventures? Might it not, on the contrary, legitimately provide the longer-term capital which a nervous, uncertain and inflation-prone capital market fails to provide? It is impossible to reconcile, in normal accounting, a flow of income or benefit in 20 to 30 years' time and a DCF, or 'present value', at an interest rate of 11 per cent. (Try it and see!)

The above remains true whether or not one uses the 'private' or some 'social' discount rate, since both are high and inflation-affected. Unless, of course, some 'real' discount rate is taken, meaning one corrected for price changes. In other words, an interest rate of 10 per cent under conditions of annual price increases of 7 per cent represents a low effective rate at fixed prices. Unfortunately, this can apply more readily to private business or householders than to nationalised industries, because of the important factor of property revaluation. We all know that the value of a house or of a commercial site appreciates, and this often shows in company accounts. A firm which borrows at 10 per cent to buy property which appreciates at 10 per cent has borrowed at a real interest rate of zero. But this hardly helps us if we are considering a power station or a gas pipe, which have to be depreciated.

A further point must be made, which may easily be over-looked. Suppose that the interest rate is high because of inflationary expectations. Then the would-be investor borrows at (say) 11 per cent to build a factory in the confident expectation that the prices of his products, when they begin to flow onto the market in five years time, will be (say) 40 per cent above present prices. I understand that nationalised industries are told not to assume inflationary price rises in future years. But if this is so, then there is an asymmetry: interest rates, ostensibly representing a social discount rate, are high because of expected price increases, yet the cash flow which they discount does not reflect these price increases.

A very different kind of objection to the whole concept of the state as the guardian of the future has been discussed by Stephen A. Marglin.[52] He views sceptically the idea that the state could or should have a view of the future different from 'individual utility functions and time-preference maps'. In particular he rejects as 'authoritarian' the notion that the government is concerned with future generations, if only because the future children cannot vote today. 'A democratic view of the state does not countenance government interference on behalf of future generations, unless the existing voters prefer to provide for the future.' He rejects also the 'schizophrenic' answer that individuals may have one set of preference in the market and another as voters; he rejects this because this assumes 'two preference maps existing side by side', and then no one can know which are the 'real' preferences and Pareto-optimality cannot be identified. He is, however, in favour of the proposition that, on certain assumptions, individuals could wish to invest in the future provided all or many others also do so, but in circumstances in which they do not or cannot wish to do so individually. In this form, he is willing to argue the existence of a social rate of discount and a social time preference different from the market rate. By this route he finally arrives at the proper conclusion, that 'the rate of interest determined in an atomistic competitive market' need *not* 'have any normative significance in the planning of collective investment.'

I have dwelt on Marglin's views because, firstly, they do

represent a formal proof, on strict welfare economics assumptions, in terms of what he calls the 'neoclassical game'. One can arrive at a 'social' rate of interest via interdependencies of individual preferences, representing a time-preference other than the market rate. My belief is that this is an ingenious and sensible way round a theoretical structure which obstructs the right road to take while rejecting the 'authoritarian' solution. However, it is perfectly feasible to accept the proposition that the electors, in a democratic process, charge the government with looking towards the future on their behalf. After all, men's time-horizon really is limited, not only by the length of their own lives but by the discount rate itself. This rate imposes a time-horizon, beyond which one need not look. It can cause us to say, as individual investors, that anything beyond 1984 is irrelevant by being beyond that horizon. But we certainly do not wish everything to stop happening in 1984! Imagine a large hydroelectric dam: do we contemplate that it should collapse after some specified future date? Suppose there are two ways of building it: one is cheaper but less durable, the other enables it to stand firm for 200 years. The former gives us higher present values at a 10 per cent discount rate. Do we not, *qua* citizens, expect the government to choose the latter on our behalf? This is not authoritarianism. It is a species of *social* time-preference, certainly. Marglin also disposes far too easily of what he calls the 'schizophrenic' argument, by treating it not in terms of *inconsistency* but in terms of two preference maps. Marglin gives the example of the man who both wants to bribe a policeman who stops him for speeding *and* favours the enforcement of the law on motorists in general. The trouble with this example is that, while certainly showing a species of schizophrenia, such a society *could* function. It would simply mean that many policemen would be bribed by many motorists, and, who knows, this outcome *might* even be preferred, as Marglin suggests. But suppose we turn to the individual who wishes to park in the street in the centre of town. He can only do so if others do not. If they all try to do so, traffic ceases to flow. These and other instances of wanting to have your cake and eat it are familiar enough. If this upsets Paretian preference

111

maps, and disrupts individual-based optima, this is because these maps and optima are artificial constructions, which require one to abstract from complementarities, indivisibilities —and inconsistencies. Indeed, how does this theory cope with a democratic vote in favour of looking after the future, or putting that Berkeley rail line underground to minimise noise, or providing a health service, or whatever? In so far as these things require raising money by taxation, or covering an operational loss by subsidy, the 'schizophrenia' argument again applies: men wish the results of taxation but prefer not to pay taxes. (Of course in the real world governments can be unrepresentative, corrupt, bureaucratic. But in the real world private business can also behave very differently from the text-book. We are for the moment in the realm of theory.)

There is a sizeable literature on all this. Henderson argues in favour of the proposition that 'collective willingness to provide for future generations is not reflected in market rates of interest, which therefore provide no guidance as to how people would wish the government to act.'[53] This represents a case for a lower rate of time-discount than the market rate. There can also be a case made for regarding the social time-preference concept with some philosophic doubt. If I decide today to build something which will be completed in five years' time, where does a time-preference discount come in? If a regional hospital board considers that it urgently needs a new geriatric hospital, and persuades the Treasury to finance it, what has time-discount to do with the reasoning behind the decision? Possibly the logical confusion arises over the handling of the time, in this case the time needed to achieve the result which we desire *today*. Also there may be a confusion between time-preference relating to the projects under discussion and the payment which an individual may expect for what Marshall called 'waiting'. If money is borrowed from me to finance a project, I would expect payment of interest at the going rate. But put yourself in the position of a socialist planner, who has become convinced for good reason that demand for housing requires enhanced production of building materials, which means that more window-glass will be needed in five years' time. The demand for housing exists now, it takes time to satisfy it, to do so will mean investment in the production of more window-glass (also bricks, cement, mortar, tiles, furniture . . .). Time-preference? In what sense does the community prefer to drink beer or play skittles today, rather than have houses tomorrow? Of course it would rather have the houses today than tomorrow, but that option is not open, for they have to be built, and that is investment. If by now the reasoning is less than clear, I can only express sympathy: theory is not very clear either. True, it could be argued that the authorities, in assessing the demand for houses or geriatric hospitals, already have a time-discount notionally in their minds. But my point remains valid: the notion of time-preference of the community, and the discount rate concept, is not unambiguous. In another of his books, Kornai shows that he too is bothered by this terminology. He approaches the problems from a different angle. He distinguishes between sacrifice, postponement and neglect. The conventional theory sees only the first: that is, we either consume today or we forego some of today's consumption in order to invest in a flow of future benefits. We discount the value of consumption in the future at the rate expressing time-preference. But Kornai points out, one can also invest 'not only at the expense of present consumption, but also at the expense of the future:' by postponing (e.g. house construction, or the building of that geriatric hospital) or by neglect (e.g. of recruiting and training of teachers) we impose burdens on the future. This, he insists, is conceptually distinct from our not consuming in the present, because what is foregone is foregone (in his example: butter not eaten over the next five years will never be eaten), whereas houses, hospitals, drainage, teachers, will in fact have to be provided later[54] (and the flow of benefits arising from their provision lasts a great deal longer than the time horizon implied by a 10 per cent discount rate!).

My imaginary opponent might argue: all this is verbiage. Capital is scarce. It should be used to the best advantage. What about opportunity cost? We must calculate.

Yes, we must indeed. But to compare a rate of return on an

opera house or an underground railway with investments in (say) real estate or copper inventories is comparing unlike with unlike, both because of considerations of cost-benefit *and* because the welfare of future generations is involved. Just as the state, as the political organ, can decide whether or not to have a national health service, so also it can choose whether to have a new line, a new non-commercial theatre, or drain marshes, build a road in the Scottish highlands, or increase the number of primary schools. Ideally these decisions should be reached by reference to their benefits to the community in relation to costs. This will be particularly important in choosing which of many projects of a similar category to select. There are bound to be arguments about what constitute benefits and how these should be weighted. Thus some would urge the importance of providing jobs at times (or in areas) of high unemployment; the alternative to a given project or subsidy might be paying men for doing nothing. There are many other considerations, and it would surely be remarkably short-sighted to exclude these things when discussing investment criteria in the state sector of the economy. Or indeed elsewhere. Thus if there is 26 per cent unemployment in the Outer Hebrides, and if shortage of capital impedes some potentially promising private industrial development, it might well make sense to subsidise, and in fact governments have done this in various forms. New devices might be tried, like a negative regional selective employment tax. But enough of this digression.

Let us return to prices. We have argued for some control, to avoid exploitation of monopoly power by nationalised enterprises. Who is to exercise this control, and on what principles? Let us leave aside the question of subsidy, i.e. selling the good or service below average cost, though this could be desirable in some cases, for reasons already argued. Let us imagine instead that we are dealing with steel, electric power or airlines, and that they ought to make a profit.

What size of profit? The Treasury has tended to lay down a norm, partly related to the investment programmes of a given industry, which (some hold) ought to be financed out of profits. This is a dubious proposition, since after all many private corporations borrow money to pay for their growth. A profit norm is a defensible principle, and some ploughing-back of profits seems entirely proper. However, a 'norm' inflexibly interpreted could lead to irrational results. Let us imagine that the electricity supply industry is told to aim for a profit rate of 18 per cent. Let us further imagine that (as happened a few years ago) it turns out that demand for electricity was overestimated, that capacity was under-utilised, and that in consequence unit costs rose above expectations. This led to a fall in profits. The principle of the profit norm would lead the management to increase prices, to try to reach the 18 per cent rate. But price increases would reduce demand (more consumers would turn to fuel oil or gas for heating), thereby ensuring, even in the medium term, an even greater under-utilisation of capacity. A vicious circle can be set into motion. It follows that a fall in profits which has an over-estimation of demand (overproduction, excess capacity) as its cause *ought* to lead to lower profits, which are the rational and logical consequence of error due to uncertainty. Lower prices may not be a feasible way out, because in the short run, the effect on demand could be negligible (one cannot instantly switch from oil to electricity for heat, for instance), while in the longer run demand would probably rise at present prices and take up the slack. Conversely, for reasons well described in Aubrey Silberston's essay[55], a short-run excess of demand over supply is often (in the real commercial world) dealt with by rationing the customers rather than by 'charging what the market can bear' in the short run, because of considerations of long-term goodwill, and therefore of longer-term demand for one's products. It is otherwise, of course, if the fall in profits is due to a rise in costs. Then, under any normal circumstances, a rise in price becomes inescapable.

So it seems reasonable to tell the management of a nationalised industry to aim at an overall profit of some broadly-indicated magnitude, and to interpret this profits 'norm' with the greatest flexibility. The same set of rules should apply to the price-controlling body: a Prices and Incomes Board, or tribunal, or ministry, or Treasury, it does not greatly matter which in principle (it might well do so in practice). They also should not be mesmerised by norms, and should try to check closely on claims that costs have increased.

The aim should be an overall profit rate. For reasons abundantly explored, *this must not and can not* mean that every segment of the given industry should be equally profitable, or profitable at all. The attempt to do this must fail and must do harm, including commercial harm. It has surely been proved several times over that any *system* of activities, the carrying out of any duties to the customers or the public, will necessarily involve some acts which are, in themselves, unprofitable. To bring marginal revenue into line with marginal costs in each instance is to chase a will o' the wisp. No private enterprise under competitive conditions can act in this way.

Should prices be varied on the basis of 'what the market can bear'? If this reflects the use of varying degrees of monopoly power, then surely this is wrong. Can we really justify a nationalised electricity industry charging more per unit merely because in a given town, gas is not available? Or because a given customer has an all-electric house? The logic of some of our economists would incline them towards freeing taxis of all price control, so that the drivers would be free to bargain, like the coachmen of old Russia (or modern London Airport, until very recently). Suppose it rains and/or there is a queue at the station, why not charge double? Unless one accepts *this* logic, one must look very carefully at the 'charge-what-the-market-can-bear' argument and its welfare implications.

Note that this is not at all the same as making charges at which supply and demand balances. It is one thing to charge more to bring peak demand down to levels which conform with available capacity, and quite another to increase fares on the London-Hull rail line because Hull happens to have no airline, even though the trains have unoccupied seats.

But what of variations in cost? Should they be totally ignored? Clearly not. A balance must be struck between standardisation of charges and adjustment to costs, especially those costs which arise out of the uneven nature of demand. Business practice differs widely, in different sectors and countries. Thus we usually expect cabbages or apples to cost more if transport and handling costs are higher, while razor blades, corn flakes and cigarettes generally cost the same in Nottingham and in northern Scotland. Consequently a nationalised industry can follow different pricing models and still be in line with the practice in many businesses. Should there be one charge for electricity, coal, steel, throughout the country? Or ought it to be varied regionally? Should Scottish coal users pay more for their coal because mines in Scotland have above-average costs? If one seeks conventional 'rationality', why stop there, why not charge different prices for deliveries from every mine, since costs do differ widely? Or, given the objects of regional policy, which are contradicted by adding to fuel bills in Scotland, should not the National Coal Board follow the razor blades and corn flakes model (and not the cabbages and apples model), and charge the same price to all users regardless of locations? Theory and precedent give one few firm guidelines, and the matter could well be decided by political considerations, not least those of regional policy. A standard charge by distance (sometimes 'tapered' as distance increases) is the rule in transport undertakings in most countries (regardless of distance within cities). The case for this, on grounds of 'system' interrelationships as well as equity, has been made earlier (pp. 31–34). It is stronger than the case for coal, in that one mine or complex of mines is not linked 'operationally' with others, in the same sense in which a transport network is a network. But in any business there are evident advantages in having prices which are predictable, clear, not excessively varied (this confuses one's own accounts almost as much as the customers) and also, I submit, non-discriminatory.

A few words about discrimination. This could mean either distinguishing between customers for the *same* thing (e.g. charging more for some than for others for transporting goods from Manchester to London, or for supplying steel under similar conditions). It could also mean varying charges as between *different* things for reasons unrelated to cost, that is, 'charging what the market will bear', and therefore charging proportionately more for a rail journey where there is no competing air service, for instance. Why, ask some, should

117

nationalised industries not be given full commercial freedom? Or, if one accepts the necessity for some control over charges, one could subject them to the approval of a supervisory body, which would accept the rightness of discriminatory charges whenever these can be shown to be good for revenue. Something like this obtained in Britain when the Prices and Incomes Board not only blessed but even advocated differential charges per mile on the railways.

Until 1953 in Great Britain discrimination in railway rates was forbidden, with some exceptions, among them a 'contract rate' which could be negotiated covering all goods belonging to one firm. But as a rule rates had to be published, and a kind of 'most-favoured-firm' clause operated: discounts granted to one firm had to be granted to others if circumstances were similar. At present, rates are secret and discrimination is normal procedure, in the name of 'commercial freedom'. This will have to be changed to conform with Common Market rules; since EEC bans variations in charges designed to aid a particular country's industries or exports, charges must be published and discrimination eliminated. They seem to have been sensible in Europe, if not necessarily for the right reasons.

Let me briefly rehearse the objections to this interpretation of proper commercial practice. It relates charges essentially to bargaining power. Big firms would get discounts, due not only to lower costs of bulk handling (which would be a legitimate reason) but simply to the effectiveness of their threat to take their custom elsewhere. The power of the nationalised industry itself, depending upon the degree of competition from substitutes, would be exerted to obtain the greatest possible leverage, i.e. it would use its monopoly or monopsonistic power whenever it had it. Logically, as already indicated, it could use this power not only to alter prices but also worsen quality, increase inconvenience, reduce durability, deny after-sales service, etc. Such actions as these do not accord with rationality even if this is conceived in a purely static, formal 'Walrasian' world. To *advocate* that the nationalised industries should have powers to act 'freely' in this whole area, merely because private monopolists in fact do so, is surely a misuse of theory and a poor

118

guide to practice. Finally, if controls are to be effectively exercised, these are bound, on practical grounds, generally to take the form of imposing some set of charges or standards of universal application. There also appear to be 'fair' to the customers, and goodwill is a matter which it does not pay to ignore.

We must now return to uneven demand. Obviously, if one were to accept that a charge per kilowatt-hour, ton or mile should apply to all customers, it does not follow that there should not be variations (applicable to all) by season or time of day. Thus it clearly pays the coal industry to have customers stock up in the summer, the transport industry to encourage the use of facilities at off-peak times. Furthermore, it can be shown to be in the general interest too, being conducive to welfare in its widest sense. It is in the nature of things that capacity required to meet peak demand will be under-used at slack periods, that the marginal cost of using it at slack periods is relatively low, and that therefore lower prices should be charged at such periods. (Here is a perfectly proper use of the word 'marginal', by the way.) Therefore off-peak tariffs, off-peak fares and the like are rational, and, surely, non-discriminatory in their nature. There are evident practical limits to such charging, of which the cost of multiple variations in charges is one. Thus the New York subways or the Paris metro would incur considerable costs if they tried to vary the fare by time of day, which probably makes it not worth while to do this. Another limit is the public's sense of right and wrong. Thus it seems, to most people, improper to charge more for electricity when the days are very cold, even though it is precisely on these days that the system is fully strained and reserve capacity (some of it doubtless obsolete and at high cost) must be brought into full operation. It is also very irritating for travellers to be told that they must pay more to travel to work at times at which they *must* travel to work, or on holidays at times when their town's factories close, and so no one (except the totally insensitive British Rail) attempts to do this. True, higher charges do help to persuade housewives to travel to town later (or would-be commuters to go by car). It is undeniable that variations in charges can lead to more efficient utilisation of capacity, though it may also worsen congestion. In any event, I am not arguing against variations of charges which reflect the peak-and-trough problem. Of course, the existence of lower off-peak charges implies that fares are higher at peak times, so it is goodwill and a good salesman's language which governs such matters to some extent. But there is a real as well as a verbal difference between levying a standard charge and offering off-peak discounts, and *adding* to the standard charges for travel at busy times, as British Rail actually do on trains to Devon and Cornwall on those summer days when the masses wish to go on holiday. This should be regarded as an improper use of monopoly bargaining power, the more so as the surcharge applies only to those routes. Admittedly, a peak surcharge is made openly for transatlantic air travel, and so could be said to be legitimate. One must not be dogmatic, and one of the decisive considerations must be what the customers consider to be right, both because the customers are the public and nationalised industries are supposed to operate in the public interest, and because goodwill is a commercial factor.

Chapter 6

Duty, Purpose, Supervision

Now to pass on to the rather vital matter of defining what needs doing, and identifying how appropriate standards should be defined. It must be clear that this will not happen automatically, that the 'commercial' criterion can stand in the way, and indeed that it must be so in so far as the nationalised industry can exercise monopolistic (or monopsonistic) power. Duty and standards need defining first of all. Whenever possible, the vague phrase 'public interest' must be given some operationally significant meaning, and an enforcement mechanism too.

There are various ways of coping with such problems, and some relevant historical experience. Thus one way is to set up independent regulatory commissions,[56] of which the Interstate Commerce Commission is an American example which still exists, and the Railway and Canal Commission was a British example. They are independent in the sense of not being part of the government, though they are appointed by the government. They could insist upon non-discrimination, standards of service and the like, and aggrieved customers could appeal to them. They have or had powers. Thus the Interstate Commerce Commission laid it down that all long-distance trains must have dining cars, and this then became an obligation binding in law. The existence of such commissions represented a recognition that private corporations exercising quasi-monopoly powers and/or franchise required supervision and regulation. It is odd that so few people realised that a public corporation working to commercial rules could equally require supervision and regulation. This could take such forms as a Nationalised Industries Commission, or separate commissions for particular industries. They would have power to issue instructions and regulations, and receive representations, including representation from the virtually powerless consumers' or users' councils, which do

121

exist in a feeble sort of way. They might also take over such residual and often ineffective powers as still reside with ministries.

Or it may be desirable on the contrary to make some of these bodies not independent but ministerial. A Ministry of Nationalised Industries could be charged with the task. Or the existing Minister of Posts and Telecommunications could discharge it *vis-à-vis* the so-called 'commercial' corporation, which now runs Britain's postal services, with neither responsibility nor supervision written into its rules.

Some constraints can take the form of legal enactments, statutory obligations, which could be guidelines for the corporation directly, as well as via supervisory bodies. Again there are historical examples. The 'Parliamentary train' has already been mentioned. So has the duty of a common carrier, or some equivalent obligation to supply any customer, perhaps at a non-discriminatory price. But specific legislation is a less flexible weapon than a law giving the necessary regulatory powers to a suitable body, which is bound to develop a species of case-law of its own regarding reasonable standards.

It is important that the supervisory body be empowered to act in the public interest, and not, like the Air Transport Licensing Board, primarily in the interest of airline revenue. Thus it would seem that the action of the Board in denying or restricting foreign airlines' landing rights at Prestwick (Scotland) airport, while undoubtedly helpful to BOAC, took little account of the interests of Scottish tourism, or indeed of the revenue of another nationalised body, the British Airports Authority, which was concerned with the under-use of this transatlantic airport.

Some may object: but would not all this detract from the responsibilities of management? Not if the task of the regulatory body is seen as setting *constraints* within which the management operates. In some cases the constraints or duties are those which a competitive market would impose: quality, punctuality, service, choice, availability, and the non-exploitation of monopoly power to the customer's detriment. The task of the supervisory body would, in effect, be to define purpose and duty, and to protect the consumer. The job will never be done perfectly; it is all too often possible to conceal slackness and to justify inflated costs. But there would be a limit more effectively set on worsening quality and service, and a customer would have a means of obtaining redress. Thus if the Post Office demands payments for retrospective charges in telephone rental charges, it could be told firmly, 'No, this is improper behaviour; we, the protectors of the public interest, will not stand for it; no competitive firm would dare do it, and therefore nor must you'.

But there is more to the public interest than imposing the equivalent of competitive conditions. We return here to the basic issue of externalities. The supervisory body would have the task of undertaking a variety of cost-benefit analyses, and either to issue appropriate orders to the public corporation itself or to report needed action to the government. A number of examples can easily be cited.

One is the problem of rural transport. There are schools which need buses to get children to them. There is the post office, which needs to deliver and collect letters. Then there are the needs of carless villagers, tourists in summer, etc. As things are, no one is responsible, and the simple expedient of a postal bus which can run also along a school route at the appropriate time can be rejected. As things are, the bus undertaking wishes to withdraw the service because it does not pay, the post office finds it convenient to run its little vans at its own times, and the education authority is left to make its own arrangements for the schoolchildren, perhaps having to spend more on boarding them out than the amount lost on the bus service. A real transport commission would have the job of eliminating this tiresome but durable nonsense, and at least would have some chance of doing so. In fact the transport of postal traffic by minibus has existed for many years in a few remote parts of the Scottish Highlands, and, at long last, it has been announced that the Post Office will adopt this idea in some other parts of Scotland too. This at least has been a positive consequence of the withdrawal of more and more of the remaining rural services operated by bus undertakings.

Still on transport, two other examples occur to me. The first concerns the widespread British habit of running trains on Sundays, and relief trains on other days, with no facilities for meals or refreshments. A commission could insist that passengers got the minimum service which a railway which took its own standards seriously would provide without specific instructions. The railway may then point out that overtime rates for catering staff are very high, and could make counter-suggestions, such as making packed lunches available, or arrange a halt for meals and drinks at a station en route, or some catering contractor going through the train. In Russia, a country hardly famed for standards of service, there was soup on trestle tables on a platform at a wayside station, since the Tallin-Moscow express had no restaurant car, and quite respectable packed lunches were available at Leningrad for travellers for Moscow. Not so if one travels on Sunday from Liverpool to Glasgow, to cite but one instance. The point is that I would visualise a dialogue: the regulating body proposes the provision of something, the regulated corporation could point out the objections (expense, and so on), and out of the discussion a solution would be arrived at, and this would be mandatory.

The other example relates to the notorious practice of British Rail to hold on to unused or derelict land and to demand a very high price for its use, usually from other public authorities. Scandalous instances of this occurred in Glasgow (Springburn) and are occurring at the time of writing in London. Appeals to Labour and Conservative governments alike elicit the response that this is within the commercial rights of British Rail. Here again the commission could investigate the rights and wrongs, aware both of the financial responsibilities of the railway and the interests of the public.

Business men, adversely affected by proposals to increase printed paper postal rates, could urge upon the appropriate supervisory body the undesirability of causing damage to exports. Thus if, as seems to be the case, it is much cheaper to post catalogues and periodicals from other countries, this affects both the printing trade and the flow of catalogues and publications. Again a little cost-benefit analysis would not be out of place. It is no one's job today to undertake it, much less to act on it.

Such a commission or ministry might also—to take another transport example—take the initiative in modernising our laws. At present the Hackney Carriage Act impedes the development of the shared taxi, which flourishes in many lands, from Turkey to Mexico, from Israel to the United States. It can be a most useful and economic urban vehicle. It can also, very valuably, provide links with stations and airports, where a bus (let alone a train) would be inflexible and too large for the job. Anyone proceeding to one of dozens of small towns near Detroit can land at Detroit airport and go to the taxi dispatcher; there he will see a list of fares and also times at which a taxi will go to (say) Ann Arbor. The dispatcher's job is to gather together everyone who is intending to go to Ann Arbor and to fill taxis, thus making the fare per person extremely reasonable. In England, this would be illegal (though the new Passenger Transport Authorities may have power to modify these rules).

There are other approaches which would supplement or perhaps replace the regulatory commission type of solution. It would be possible to devise indicators to measure 'quality' in some way. Example: since no one desires electricity profits to be earned through underproviding peak-load capacity, profits could be notionally reduced whenever load-shedding or power cuts occur (without lawful excuse, for example strikes, or other kinds of force). Another example: the number of standing passengers on long-distance trains, or the number of individuals who fail to get on trains, or unpunctuality, ought all to be included in a computation of managerial efficiency in a rail service. It is, of course, a hard task to put numbers to such considerations, and so these ideas may not be practicable in such crude form, but that which cannot be precisely quantified does not cease to be real. We do *not* want nationalised (or any other) industries to achieve their financial objectives at the cost of their customers' convenience, or rather we certainly would wish to ensure that the many uses and abuses of monopoly power are checked. This is sometimes achieved by imposing standards or legal duties, perhaps more often by or through a supervisory body. It is a matter of empirical study. What is essential is to appreciate the nature of the problem, otherwise no solution will even be sought.

There have been instances of the public corporation being, in its turn, denied development rights by another public authority. A notorious instance was Euston Station, which would have had a highly remunerative office block built above it, but planning permission was refused by the local authority. There have also been repeated instances of nationalised industries (the railways especially) seeking in vain to secure Treasury or Ministry approval for an investment, which was denied on the grounds, no doubt, that the taxpayer might have to foot some part of the bill. In doing so, they applied the 'fragmented' analysis which we have criticised in earlier pages. So it is not by any means always the case that the public authority exercises powers wisely *vis-à-vis* nationalised industries. In fact, Christopher Foster has quoted numerous instances in which, paradoxically, the nationalised industry was advocating the public interest and it was the supervisory ministry which was trying to impose profitability criteria.[57] Stewart Joy, of British Rail, in an unpublished paper complains strongly of excessive and petty supervision over project choice. Henderson takes, rightly, the view that public-sector managers should take a broad view of their objectives, and remarked that 'it would be foolish to confine the choice of senior appointments to those who are prepared to deny themselves this freedom' (to consider issues wider than profitability).[58] Indeed this is so, and it reminds one of the importance of so defining the function of management of nationalised industries that they themselves keep the public interest in mind.

To use an earlier illustration again, if razor-blade manufacturers were nationalised, one should expect the management to wish that the blades shave smoothly and well, and so to hesitate before making blades blunter to fulfil a profit norm. British Rail should be ashamed of closing so many freight depots and sidings that they compel loads to be despatched by large lorries, which create additional congestion. (It may not be all that good for their business either.) It is out of its own everyday decisions that such consequences follow, therefore its management, like that of other nationalised industries, should certainly be instructed to bear in mind the external effects of its actions, and not only the impact on its profit-and-loss account. If the cost looks large, then naturally it would be its duty to bring this to the attention of the ministry. But the consequences of action or inaction are more likely to be identified, and the costs of alternatives computed, by the management rather than by the ministry. Stress should be laid on so-called social objectives as part of managerial responsibility. The ministry (or other supervisory body) must itself be re-educated if it is to carry out its job in the public interest; this much is clear from the evidence cited by both Foster and Joy. However, it is also the case that petty day-to-day supervision can be demoralising to management, so it is also a question of correctly drafting its terms of reference. Nonetheless, an effective supervisory body, stronger than consumers' consultative committees, is highly desirable.

Harm has been done by the constant reiteration, in recent years, of the 'commercial' principle, for then the little men who take routine everyday decisions can be (unconsciously) encouraged to neglect the welfare of the customer. Thus if railway officials expected to be reprimanded if they failed to get the passengers away, they might take the trouble to do so. It is not the managing director who decides not to run an extra train or bus to deal with a holiday crowd on a fine weekend on the Clyde coast; for the local superintendent the extra cost may seem unjustified, if the accounts, rather than service, are for ever in his mind. There may indeed be 'goodwill' effects of good service, which would manifest themselves in ways invisible to the local official.

It is no source of pride in the economic profession to note that, in the discussions of the Select Committee on Nationalised Industries in 1968, only one man seriously raised the issue of the meaning of 'commercial' in the context of nationalisation, and that this one man was A. H. Hanson, a political scientist.

Some economists, faced with problems of quality and service, are apt to think not of enforcement mechanisms but of choice. 'People should have what they pay for.' Yes, but in many instances the element of choice is absent; if a goods depot is closed, or weekend postal deliveries are not provided, there is no choice. Also this abstracts from the misuse of monopoly power in a bargaining situation in circumstances in which some choice does exist.

One can visualise at this point a chorus of Chicago economists, conducted perhaps by Milton Friedman, and the burden of their song would be, 'Let a market do the job, and thereby avoid the pitfalls both of nationalised monopoly and of bureaucratic devices to mitigate its inherent evils'.

The short answer is that the market can indeed be the answer, subject to two provisos. One relates to the presence of appreciable externalities, the other to so-called natural monopolies (telephones, electricity and the like), or even perhaps to 'unnatural' monopolies, those which have in fact arisen and take socially undesirable forms. It is certainly not my task to argue 'against the market'. However, at the very beginning of the paper care was taken to associate nationalisation with conditions to which the pure free market solution is *not* appropriate.

It is also worth stressing that some forms of competition, while attractive as a measure of offering 'choice', in fact can operate to the disadvantage of the consumer and of society. These cases relate to instances where choice is restricted by circumstances to a handful of possible suppliers. Two examples will suffice. The first is television. It is easy to demonstrate that programmes presented by (say) three competing companies are very likely to offer the viewer *less* choice than three programmes presented by one corporation.[59] The second is less obvious, but to my mind can be equally conclusive, and concerns transport. Suppose that one is considering services between Liverpool and Manchester, or Munich and Nürnberg. If trains *and* buses were to run in competition, there would be empty seats on some trains and, owing to the high overheads, costs per passenger-mile would rise. There would be a strong temptation to curtail the service or not to introduce better or more comfortable trains. This would not matter if buses were perfect substitutes for trains, but they are not. Thus heavy luggage cannot be carried on buses, they are slower, they are more likely to be halted by snow (an important consideration in Germany), and they are less able to cope with peak-load traffic. It may well be that the best solution for the customer is to deprive him of 'choice' and not to have express buses between these points, if this is the precondition of an efficient rail service.

In other cases the existence of competition can simply lead to a total withdrawal of the rail service. For example, suppose Lowestoft, or Scarborough, or Falmouth, were told that the choice was either to close the loss-making railway or to eliminate the competing bus. They could well choose to have no choice, in so far as they would benefit from those special features of railways which the bus could not reproduce (speed, connections, holiday traffic, and so on). Such a decision, if taken, could only be taken by a political process, local or national. The need for this arises from indivisibility: a railway line either exists or it does not exist.

There is something of an analogy here with the inherent limitations of competition in television, already mentioned above. A public authority with a duty to provide a good service might well be able to perform better without competition. A German example is the route from Munich to the mountain resort of Oberammergau. Passengers go by train to a junction at a place called Murnau. Thence the railway runs a bus at slack periods, trains at busy times, and in winter the train is more likely to run than the bus. The beneficiaries of this arrangement include the skiers of Munich and the hotel-keepers of Oberammergau. Competing buses would probably have destroyed the rail service, to no very obvious advantage. It is, at least, somebody's responsibility (the Deutsche Bundesbahn's, no doubt, supervised by the Ministry of Transport) to inquire into the circumstances of the case and decide the best way to link Oberammergau with Bavarian cities. The decision could, of course be wrong. But it can be deliberately taken by an authority responsible for providing an adequate service;

through bookings and connections come logically within its purview.

I have before me the British Rail timetable for Scotland, which does now at least contain the times of some buses, but at the bottom of each page one sees the following legend: 'This information is inserted for the convenience of the public, and the Publishers are not responsible for the accuracy of the said information, nor do they guarantee the coaches or motors. . . . The respective proprietors advertise that the above services run in connection with British Rail.'[60] It is thereby almost militantly made clear that British Rail takes *no* responsibility. Perhaps this is why, according to Table 88 of this timetable, passengers on the service from Orkney to Scrabster are transported to Thurso railway station by a bus timed to arrive at 11.45, to 'connect' with a train due to leave over $5\frac{1}{2}$ hours later at 17.23, the previous train being timed to leave precisely 18 minutes before the arrival of the 'connecting' bus. This is only one small example of the effect of separate ownership or control upon the coordination of transport services.

Yet Alan Day sees no better solution than encouraging *more* competition between road and rail, by removing existing restrictions on the number of buses running on long distance routes. While some of these restrictions may well be obsolete or indefensible, his proposals seem to show no awareness of the negative consequences which competition can produce, especially where traffic is light and there is indivisibility. Another recent Scottish example concerns the competition between the MacBraynes and Western Ferries boats to Islay and Jura. The latter, privately owned, specialise on car ferry work; they use boats which cause difficulties in rough weather, have few facilities for small package traffic which is so important to the islanders, operate no bus connection on the mainland, and, on top of all this, do not call at certain ports on the islands, compelling the residents there to incur the inconvenience of fetching their cargoes and visitors. Western Ferries undercut MacBrayne's rate for cars and took most of this traffic. The effect was to persuade the present government to transfer to Western Ferries the state subsidy for the route; MacBraynes (a

subsidiary of the nationalised Scottish Transport Group)
promptly announced the withdrawal of its service. Net result,
in terms of a cost benefit analysis, is almost certainly a worsening of the service. Professor Day should realise that such
things are not necessarily beneficial.

Chapter 7

Theory, Nationalised Industries and Socialism

Where has all this discussion taken us?

Firstly, I hope that it has convinced most readers tha 'commercial' operation of nationalised industries raises a host o problems which are now, as a rule, swept under the carpet o ignored. No one was more guilty of ignoring them than the Labour governments under Harold Wilson, or had less excuse for doing so, since Labour ought to be thinking seriously abou how to make nationalisation contribute to some social purpose It is paradoxical to find the Conservative government unde Heath, contrary to its ideology and professions, considerin loss-making activities by nationalised industries as one means o reducing unemployment.

Secondly, some readers will have grasped the limitations o disembodied, one-dimensional marginalism, of the so-calle 'theory of the firm' which purports to relate to real firms bu does not do so. Also how some real-world errors arise out o misconceived or misinterpreted theory.

Thirdly, something useful has surely been said about invest ment criteria, perhaps convincing some that a theory derivec from statistics and applicable (if at all) to a competitive worl of small firms, takes on a rather different meaning if applied t whole industries under uncertainty.

Fourthly, a blow might have been struck in favour of regard ing institutions, the organisation of decision-making, as highl germane to resource allocation, in nationalised and privat business alike. Organisational economies of scale matter.

Fifthly, some useful correctives may have been made to narrowly conceived monopoly theory, and its misapplication t nationalised industries has led to serious misunderstanding.

132

Sixthly, the observant reader might be saved from naivety on the subject of subsidies in general, 'cross-subsidisation' in particular.

Seventhly, systems analysis must surely be brought to bear on micro-economic theory, with all that this implies in the form of complementarities, margins within margins, and sub-systems within systems. Here too is the problem of sub-optimisation, which has a direct bearing on our understanding of centralisation and decentralisation within a western corporation (private or nationalised) and within a socialist economy. If this requires us to go well beyond the one-dimensional world of simplified welfare economics and Pareto-optimality, then it is about time we did just that.

Lastly, externalities will have perhaps been lifted out of footnotes and into their proper place. To contemplate nationalised industries, above all, and relegate externalities to insignificance is a nonsense. Maybe this should be set in a wider context. We live in a world in which pollution, conservation, congestion, unemployment and regional imbalance matter more and more. We get in each other's way on an overcrowded planet. 'Yet it has been left rather to the natural scientists to sound the alarm, while orthodox economists, unperturbed, continue to elaborate the presumption in favour of *laissez-faire*.'[61] What we do in pursuit of private profit *can* do others harm. We may know that this is so, but we persist in an economic theory which assumes that the hidden hand will ensure the concordance of micro-profitability with the common weal. I accept that such concordance frequently exists, and also that institutional attempts to 'catch' all externalities can be expensive and ineffective. However, what once could perhaps be regarded as exceptions to the general 'market' rule must by now be regarded as far too important to be left on the outside edge of theory. Great private corporations replace the market by internal administration, yet we persist in having nationalised industries whose management's terms of reference deny the very objects of nationalisation. 'Commercial' principles, which belong to a pre-corporation age, stand in the way even of 'internal economies', (the commercial interest of the public corporation itself), let alone a necessary concern for those very numerous cases in which sectional profit and public interest can contradict each other.

As already argued at length, externality is a matter of organisation and responsibility. The question must be asked: external to whom? This question arises in discussion of decentralisation, whether in a socialist economy or in a great private corporation. Where there are strong elements of system, of interdependencies, conventional 'marginal' analysis tends to miss the point, and there could be a strong case for internalising externalities, by substituting administered relations for market relations.

'Conventional' micro-economics could do with a strong dose of reality, and cease to evade it by recourse to higher mathematics, unless the mathematics are helpful in comprehending and generalising it, of course.

'Economists have been relatively uninterested in descriptive micro-economics. . . . The classical economic theory of markets with perfect competition is deductive theory which requires almost no contact with empirical data once its assumptions are accepted.'[62] No one brought up so should advise on criteria appropriate to any industry in the real world.

Let me repeat that properly understood micro-economics does not *contradict* the arguments here presented. No doubt critics and reviewers would have no difficulty in pointing to examples which show that most of the points raised in these pages have been made somewhere, by economists in or close to the mainstream. No one advocates that interdependencies be ignored. There is a sizeable literature on externalities. Even the 'purest' neo-classical theorists are aware of the existence of large corporations. It is largely a question of emphasis, or perhaps of blinkers which are inadvertently worn by many who are conventionally brought up. Some matters are neglected, because of the nature of the simplifying assumptions which are commonly made.

It is possible that micro-economics ought to remain essentially 'incrementalist' and one-dimensional, and that systems and industry-wide analysis falls logically into another branch of the subject, situated midway between macro- and micro-economics: *mezzo-economics*. Here would 'belong' problems of monopoly and monopsony, of economic power and input-output tables, of organisational charts, international firms, decision-making within hierarchies and such phenomena as 'satisficing' and sub-optimisation, and also complementarities and the like. None of these things are within the purview of macro-economics. None of them fit into the Pareto-Walras approach, which concerns small units operating in markets within which competition takes the form of men crying their wares and prices out loud. There is room in economics for the perfect competition hypothesis and for models based upon it. There is scope also for 'mezzo-economics', which appears to have bearing upon nationalised industries and their problems because of its emphasis on systems of inter-relationships, institutional factors and multi-dimensionality, within which margins and marginal analysis do have their proper place, in the context of systems.

Two 'unorthodox' supporters can be quoted at this point with profit. First, Joan Robinson. 'The function of economic theory, as opposed to economic theology, is to set up hypotheses that can be tested. But if an hypothesis is framed in terms of a position of equilibrium that would be attained if all parties concerned had correct foresight, there is no point in testing it: we know in advance that it will prove correct.' And again: 'There is an irresistible attraction about the concept of equilibrium—the silent hum of a perfectly running machine. . . . We have to look for a psychological explanation to account for the influence of an idea that is intellectually unsatisfactory.'[63] The second is from the invaluable Janos Kornai, who puts with force and eloquence a view with which I am in evident sympathy. 'The multi-level phenomena of social life and especially the hierarchy of administration, control and bureaucracy have engaged the attention of a whole series of sociologists since the time of Max Weber. It is surprising that economics should have neglected for so long the problem of multi-level phenomena, especially given the analogies provided by other branches of science.'[64]

Let me again stress that it is not here asserted that British (or y other) nationalised industries are inefficient, or more efficient than private industry. Anyone can make mistakes, and frequently does. Many nationalised industries do very well. It is hard, however, to resist the conclusion that this is often despite the advice received from economists, or the lessons drawn (sometimes admittedly wrongly drawn) from economic theory.

What lessons can be drawn from the preceding pages which might serve to clarify economic problems of socialism? This is no place for an analysis of the many meanings of 'socialism'. Comment will be confined to two aspects. First of all, let us consider how a moderate social-democratic or labour party, operating within a largely capitalist environment, could look at the matter. Secondly, it is worth devoting rather more pages to the all-inclusive state economies of the East.

An economic adviser to the Labour party might put a case as follows. There is no point in nationalising any industry which is operating under reasonably competitive conditions. Is there any point in nationalising quasi-monopolies, such as the chemical or sugar giants, unless powerful special reasons for doing so exist? What could such reasons be?

One, of course, would be their failure to grow, or a threatened bankruptcy. A second is that they should be operated in the public interest. However, as we have seen, this raises awkward problems, both of definition and administration. It is in the public interest that they be operated efficiently. Open-ended subsidisation can lead to waste of resources on an intolerable scale. It is, of course, possible to urge nationalised enterprises to operate in a competitive environment. Competition can be *between* nationalised industries (for example, coal, gas and electricity in Great Britain), or between nationalised firms and private firms in the *same* industry (such as the Renault and the Simca car plants in France). Under these conditions, nationalised management does have a powerful impetus towards efficiency.

The idea of competition *between* the nationalised and private sectors was part of the 'philosophy' of NEP (the New Economic Policy) in Russia in the early 'twenties. The intention was that large-scale industry and trade would gradually overcome the private sector in economic struggle, by their ability to deliver the goods better and cheaper.[65] In fact, the destruction of the private sector was completed by a mixture of police measures and penal taxation, but the idea itself should not be unattractive to some socialists. Given that a fully-fledged state monopoly in any sector can develop regrettable tendencies towards substituting *bürokratische Bequemlichkeit* for dynamism or concern for consumer interest, why not allow challenge from 'privateers' where this is feasible? (In Warsaw there are private, as well as state, taxis; in Budapest restaurants are leased to private operators, to give two contemporary 'eastern' examples.) In Britain there has been a tendency to nationalise a *whole* industry or not at all.[66] Perhaps there is scope for the 'French car' or mixed model.

In such cases, the bulk of the questions we have been discussing here might well solve themselves, without supervisory measures, through the normal disciplines of competition. One does not have to tell Renault to provide reliable service and punctual deliveries, because its customers could go elsewhere. A possible scenario for such nationalisation might be, for instance, the threatened closure of a major car firm or shipyard group, and nationalisation would then be justified in terms of maintaining employment and of regional policy. Socialists could argue that nationalisation would have positive effects on efficiency and the morale of the labour force. They could then be proved right, or wrong, by results.

However, as was pointed out at the beginning, Labour's case for nationalisation usually relates to sectors within which competition is either impracticable or undesirable, and is also (or should also be) concerned with social-economic externalities. It is unnecessary to repeat here what has been said earlier (perhaps too often), that Labour's thinking on how those nationalised quasi-monopolies should be run requires, indeed demands, a new look. *Only* by a stress on public service, on the general interest, can one make sense of the nationalisation 'plank' in Labour's programme. 'Make a reality of cost-benefit analysis' may not be a good election slogan, but it would make sense as a principle.

Private firms can only concern themselves with private benefits. Public enterprises, told to concern themselves with their profit and loss accounts, will also neglect public benefit. It has, I hope, been amply demonstrated that, to the extent that competition is absent, this neglect will often 'pay'. The necessity of cost-consciousness, with full awareness of opportunity-cost, must therefore coexist with the institutional means of assessing those benefits (and costs) which fall outside the accounts of the enterprise concerned. Unless this is done, the public will become increasingly aware that nationalisation and neglect of the public go together, and this cannot be good for Labour's image and morale. It would also seem wrong for Labour to accept the idea that investment criteria should be identical in the public and private sectors. Logically this entails the proposition that ownership makes no difference to the outcome, in which case why bother to change ownership? It reminds me of Ramsay MacDonald's days, when Labour sought to prove that it was 'fit to govern' by doing very much what the Conservatives would have done.

But it is perhaps more interesting to contemplate the relevance of the ideas here advanced to socialist economies of the Soviet pattern. Before doing this, the reader must be made aware of the existence of several attitudes or viewpoints towards socialist planning, each of which in turn has a number of variants. These are represented by the following institutions or ideas.

(a) The Soviet centralised model, which is based on central assessment of need and on 'directive' planning, in which this assessment is translated into action by a system of instructions via an economic-political hierarchy. Criteria for management are predominantly related to the fulfilment of the directive plans.

(b) The 'market socialist' model, one form of which was evolved in the late 'thirties by Lange and Lerner. Other forms exist in Yugoslavia (in association with 'workers' self-management'), and also in Hungary. Current output plans are made by managers in negotiation with their customers. Central plans relate to major investments, or use fiscal (or price-control) rather than 'directive' methods to attain desired goals. Soviet reformers have been urging similar changes in the USSR, so far with little success.

(c) The 'New Left' purism, which attacks *both* the Soviet centralised model, for bureaucracy, privilege and conservatism, *and* the market-socialists for revisionism. For the typical New Left critic, market and socialism are incompatible. Socialism is production for use, not production for the market. Prices and market criteria stand in the way of the assessment of real social-economic advantage.[67]

(d) The anti-socialist view, expressed in a variety of ways by Barone, Mises, Hayek, Robbins and many others. It has been frequently asserted that (a) is inefficient and (c) impracticable. Some welcome (b) as a sign of 'convergence', others deny its feasibility in the absence of a capital market.

All these views, and their many variants, raise far more problems than can be discussed here. Let me just recapitulate the points which arise in the present context.

Firstly, as already noted, the centralised model in fact decomposes itself into departments, ministries, divisions, into a kind of administrative pluralism. This is an inevitable consequence of the sheer scale of detailed work which is thrust upon the centre by the very nature of the model. In theory it might seem that the centralisation of decision-making ensures that all is considered by reference to all, in an economy-wide cost-benefit analysis. But this cannot happen. The total replacement of market relations by administration is not only costly, it creates problems which are of their nature insoluble. Or it may be better to speak of 'vast diseconomies of scale'. Inter-departmental demarcation lines, bureaucratic barriers and sub-optimisation are inescapable.

If each micro-decision is part of the central plan, if output, inputs, deliveries, labour wages and investments are to be decided by what is sometimes airily called the 'Central Planning Board', then the number of such decisions runs into many quadrillions. The computer cannot resolve the resulting computation bottlenecks, simply because it would take far too long to collect the information and to convert it into programmes which computers can handle. It is the impossibility of handling this vast flow of data, and administering the innumerable inter-linkages of which the system is composed, which gives rise to familiar deficiencies of centralised planning: administrative fragmentation, difficulties of coordination, inconsistent plans, adaptation of the product mix to aggregated plan targets instead of to user requirements, departmental 'competition' for investment grants, and so on. The attempt to eliminate externalities by trying to administer the whole economy as one firm is necessarily self-defeating, with administrative-departmental boundary lines replacing those created, under capitalism, by separate ownership.

The experience of Stalinist planning, as already noted, drives reformers in Eastern Europe towards the market solution. They are denounced both by the supporters of the centralised model and by the 'New Left'.

The latter, by attacking the market, logically put themselves in the position of advocating the substitution, in micro-economic affairs, of the visible for the hidden hand. They have as yet given no answer to the rather obvious counter-attack; the visible hand can only operate in the form of a highly complex administrative machine, which must surely generate most of the bureaucratic-centralist distortions of Soviet experience. Who but the centre, in a modern industrial society, would be able to decide between ends, means and alternative uses if no market-and-price mechanism exists? The usual answer is to denounce the USSR as not socialist, and assert the virtues of democracy and workers' control. Workers' self-management *à la* Yugoslavia is, however, only conceivable in a market environment. Without a market the elected committee would have to take instructions from the central planners, who alone will have the necessary information about ends and means.

Some of the new left envisage a prolonged transition period to a real socialism, or full communism, where markets, prices and wages will disappear in a world of abundance; 'to each according to his needs'. However, it is not with this perhaps Utopian world that we, or East European reformers, are concerned.

The Chinese economy may appear to represent a middle way,

with considerable decentralisation to communes and localities, but this may well be due primarily to the still primitive and local nature of much of the Chinese economy, which enables them to confine central planning to the relatively small and 'manageable' modern industrial sector.

Yet the critics of the 'market' reformers do have a point. Some reformers seem to be so impressed by the need to eliminate bureaucratic centralism that they pay little attention to externalities, economies of scale and the many other matters discussed in this book.

Perhaps a good way of looking at the problem is to imagine oneself with the task of redesigning the whole structure of economic management. This is not an impossible idea. There is at this moment a kind of Grand Committee on economic structure in Warsaw, trying to hammer out a feasible reform of the Polish economy.

Surely, one might begin by recognising that there would clearly have to be some decentralisation; that *any* decentralisation (or indeed any division of centralised functions between departments) gives rise to fragmentation of the economy; that in some degree the whole economy is a system; and that consequently a sub-optimisation problem will arise. This same problem arises in any consideration of devolution of authority in any organisation, whether economic, political, military or academic. To centralise adds to cost, and sometimes detracts from the quality of the decision itself. Thus, the more that has to be decided at the centre of a large organisation, the greater is the delay, the remoteness (and perhaps unclarity of vision), and the more likely it is that the decision will be taken by an underling working with a rule-book, and by precedent. But whatever decisions are taken about how future decisions are to be taken they will affect what is decided in some degree.

If this is so, one can set about drawing up ideas concerning industrial sectors, and types of problem too, where it is reasonable to expect the advantages of centralisation to outweigh the disadvantages, and *vice versa*. One would note that electricity generation is a 'plannable' industry, with homogeneous output, predictable inputs, interlinked power stations and good, unambiguous communications. Investments would depend decisively on computations best made at the centre, about technical progress and the intentions of consumers and developments of alternative fuels. Cabbage, women's skirts, confectionery, instruments and implements are more likely to benefit from flexible market-type relationships between producers and users. My colleague, J. G. Zielinski, pointed out that if Polish planners forgot about some minor item like pickled cucumbers (or clothes-pegs, or pins), these things were not available at all.[68] This too is an argument for flexibility, provided under capitalism by private enterprise, and under Soviet-type socialism perhaps by producers' cooperatives working for the market under competitive conditions.

Similarly, one could envisage certain questions being reserved for corporations or the central planners. Very large investment projects, for instance, probably including those affecting cabbages, women's skirts or even cucumbers, but not including questions relating to the number or shape of the secretaries working at the Electricity Board headquarters.

A formal statement of the problem could well be based on the conception of parallel 'hierarchies' of margins and organisations. Whenever a marginal decision affects only the level at which it is taken, or where the cost of referring the matter upwards would exceed the benefit derived from doing so, the decision can best be taken at that level. One then builds up a multi-level structure, in which there are many kinds of subunits, divisions, firms, corporations or trusts, industry-wide organs and finally national planning agencies. Just as the degree of decentralisation, and the role of competition, would vary greatly according to sector, and to the subject-matter and scale of the decisions being taken, so also one can envisage a variety of operational criteria and of supervisory agencies (in non-competitive sectors) to enforce standards of quality and service.

So a real optimum will involve institutional variety, a reconciliation of conflicting desiderata in respect of flexibility, local knowledge and the avoidance of bureaucratic structures on the one hand, and the need to take externalities into account on the other. Socialist theorists, like business consultants for western corporations, must try to identify what the Russians call 'local optima', that is procedures by which decentralised decision-makers respond to criteria (price, profit, or some other measure of satisfaction of consumer requirements) in such a way as to contribute to an overall optimum. A real optimum, outside textbook perfectionism, must be defined as the best which it is *feasible* to achieve. Perfect organisation is as impossible as perfect competition. Thus experience teaches that *any* planning structure based upon industrial sectors will have weaknesses in its regional policies, whereas a structure based upon regions will inevitably develop weaknesses in dealing with the common problems of industrial sectors (as was seen in the USSR during the Khrushchev experiment with regional economic councils).

Similarly in the British nationalised sector it seems right and necessary to aim at operational autonomy and unambiguous commercial criteria, but for reasons discussed at great length already, these aims conflict with other considerations.

It has been my contention that theory has misled; above all it has misled by silence. Silence about many of its own restrictive and unrealistic assumptions. Silence about many of the problems most directly relevant to large organisations in the modern world. Definitions are left vague, on matters as important to the theory as margins, maximisation, optimum and production possibilities frontier. Self-contradictory phrases such as 'competitive equilibrium' remain in textbooks for a generation and more.

In a world of huge units, most of us persist in talking of competitive markets, although, as everyone knows, oligopoly is prevalent. In the words of John S. Chipman, 'the competitive price mechanism cannot be expected to provide a stable framework under conditions of oligopoly'. Indeed the principle of maximisation 'becomes meaningless, since nobody knows what he can maximise and nobody knows what are the constraints'.[69] Shubik has argued that we have in effect *no* theory of oligopoly, and Koopmans that we cannot effectively handle uncertainty. Yet people teach, and give advice, as if the world of Walras and

143

Pareto was not one of abstract and ingenious theorising, but bore some relation to reality. How else can one explain the disease of vulgarmarginalist fragmentation, to which economists have made a notable contribution? Some of these economists are probably supporters of the Labour party, sincerely anxious that nationalised industries conform to the principles of efficient operation as they conceive them. Of course, we cannot blame them, or theory, for not finding speedy and painless ways of solving the complex problems of this or that industry.

Theory cannot possibly begin to go into the very varied operational details with which the practitioners must concern themselves. All that we can ask is that, in abstracting from them, the theorists do not blind themselves, or their students, to the existence of the complications with which life abounds.

Reference Notes

1 Some of these were, or are, run by municipalities, but these too are *public* authorities.
2 E. J. Mishan, *Twenty-one Popular Economic Fallacies* (Allen Lane, 1969).
3 This also abstracts from multiplier (cumulative) effects of employing, or ceasing to employ, large numbers of labourers.
4 K. Lancaster, 'A new approach to consumer theory', *Journal of Political Economy*, Volume 74 (1960).
5 Of course in practice there are substitutes, and so no monopoly, public or private, can be regarded as complete.
6 In fact, many quasi-monopolies energetically increase output and are good at keeping down costs. Experience varies.
7 Subsidies for 'unprofitable' routes will be discussed later.
8 Actually, they used to decrease fares selectively, which is a less objectionable way of achieving the desired object; more of this later.
9 They are paid a sum from the social insurance funds for this.
10 *First Report from the Select Committee on Nationalised Industries*, Volume II (Minutes of evidence) (HMSO, London, 1968), p. 619. Emphasis mine.
11 William G. Shepherd, 'Cross-subsidisation in coal', in R. Turvey (ed.), *Public Enterprise* (Penguin, 1971), p. 348.
12 Joan Robinson, *Economic Heresies* (Macmillan, 1971), p. 141.
13 M. Shubik, 'A curmudgeon's view of micro-economics', *Journal of Economic Literature*, (June 1970).
14 G. B. Richardson, *Information and Investment* (O.U.P., London, 1960).
15 J. Kornai, *Anti-equilibrium* (North Holland Publishing Company, Amsterdam, 1971), p. 9.
16 Oscar Lange, the Polish economist, recommended this as the rule for socialist enterprises in his celebrated pre-war article.
17 Shubik, op. cit., p. 413.
18 Joan Robinson, *Economic Heresies* (Macmillan, 1971), p. 56.
19 *Cahiers de l'ISEA* No. 130, (October, 1962), p. 52.
20 Shepherd, op. cit., p. 328.
21 'Internal economies', *Economic Journal*, (December 1969).
22 Jack Wiseman shows a proper scepticism about marginal cost pricing. See his 'Theory of public utility price-an empty box', *Oxford Economic Papers*, (1957).
23 In Bolivia everyone has to fetch letters from and take letters to the post office. There are neither deliveries nor collections. In La Paz there is only one post office!
24 Kornai, op. cit., p. 339.
25 Robert Heller in the *Observer*, (7 May 1972), p. 16.
26 Kornai, op. cit., p. 353.
27 *See* A. Nove, 'Planners preferences, priorities and reforms', *Economic Journal* (June 1966).
28 Kornai, op cit., p. 148.
29 *Ekonomika i organizatsiya promyshlennogo proizvodstva* No. 6 (1971), p. 7. Emphasis his.

30 *Ibid.* Emphasis his.

31 *Ibid.*, p. 22.

32 *Ibid.*, p. 32.

33 Kornai, op. cit., p. 201.

34 W. S. Ryan, *Network Analysis in Forming a New Organisation*, C.A.S. Occasional Paper No. 3 (HMSO, London, 1967), p. 3.

35 Other motives will be discussed later.

36 It is in a satire on *university* administration that Cornford wrote his classic words, 'Anything that does not already exist is a dangerous precedent; therefore nothing must ever be done for the first time.'

37 Even professors have them, so rumour has it. This is pure theory, of course.

38 P. D. Henderson, 'Investment criteria for public enterprises', in R. Turvey (ed.), *Public Enterprise* (Penguin, 1971). pp. 126–7.

39 *Ibid.*, p. 415.

40 *Ibid.*, p. 441.

41 H. Arndt, 'Economic theory of power' in Arndt (ed.), *Die Konzentration in der Wirtschaft* (Duncker & Humblot, Berlin, 1971) pp. 100–136. Copy kindly sent to me by the author. (The previous paragraph was written *before* receiving Arndt's paper. Evidently some minds think alike.)

42 Arndt, op. cit., pp. 120–2.

43 *Sunday Times* (19 September 1971).

44 Shepherd, op. cit., p. 348.

45 Henderson, op. cit., pp. 126, 131.

46 Joan Robinson, in *On Political Economy and econometrics* (essays in honour of Oskar Lange) (Warsaw, 1964), pp. 518–9.

47 H. A. Simon, 'Decision-making in economics', in *Surveys of Economic Theory*, Volume 3, p. 2.

48 *Three Essays on the State of Economic Science* (New York, McGraw Hill, 1957), p. 147. Emphasis mine.

49 G. B. Richardson, 'Planning versus competition', *Soviet Studies* (January 1971), pp. 456–7.

50 C. J. Hitch, *Operations Research*, 1960, pp. 443–4.

51 S. Joy, 'Pricing and investment in railway freight services', *Transport Economics and Policy*, Volume 5, No. 3 (Sept. 1971), pp. 1–16. (My copy may be an early version of the paper, in which case I apologise to Mr Joy for using a manuscript which perhaps was not intended for quotation).

52 *Quarterly Journal of Economics* (February 1963).

53 Henderson, op. cit., p. 98.

54 J. Kornai, *Rush versus Harmonic Growth* (North Holland Publishing Company, Amsterdam, 1972), pp. 69–75.

55 *Economic Journal* (September 1970).

56 One of my first jobs was to act as research assistant to, and draft a chapter for, Robert E. Cushman of Cornell, who was preparing his book *Independent Regulatory Commissions* (New York, O.U.P., 1941).

57 C. Foster, *Politics, Finance and the Role of Economics* (Allen & Unwin, 1972).

58 Henderson, op. cit., p. 131.

59 See P. Wiles, 'Pilkington', *Economic Journal* (June, 1963).

60 This, by the way, is not even true. Only certain services, on certain of the routes referred to, claim to do this.

61 Robinson, op. cit., p. 55.

Reference Notes

62 Simon, op. cit., p. 19.
63 Joan Robinson *Economic Philosophy* (Pelican, 1970), pp. 70, 77–8.
64 Kornai, op. cit., p. 84.
65 In addition, state trusts competed with each other, at least until 1926.
66 Odd exceptions exist, or existed, such as the Carlisle pubs. There were also interesting instances of municipal enterprise.
67 See A. Nove 'Market socialism and its critics', *Soviet Studies*, (July 1972), and the works of C. Bettelheim and P. Sweezy there referred to.
68 J. G. Zielinski, *Economic Reforms in Polish Industry* (OUP) (forthcoming).
69 J. S. Chipman, 'The nature and meaning of equilibrium in economic theory' in H. Townsend (ed.), *Price Theory* (Penguin, 1971), pp. 368, 369.

Index

149